HOT RODS & CUSTOM CARS

HOT RODS & CUSTOM CARS

GENERAL EDITOR: CRAIG CHEETHAM

MOTORBOOKS
INTERNATIONAL

This edition published in 2004 by
Motorbooks International,
an imprint of MBI Publishing Company,
Galtier Plaza, Suite 200,
380 Jackson Street,
St. Paul, MN 55101-3885
United States

The information in this book is true and complete to the best of our knowledge. All recommendations are made without any guarantee on the part of the author or Publisher, who also disclaim any liability incurred in connection with the use of this data or specific details.

We recognize that some words, model names and designations, for example, mentioned herein are the property of the trademark holder. We use them for identification purposes only. This is not an official publication.

Motorbooks International titles are also available at discounts in bulk quantity for industrial or sales-promotional use. For details write to Special Sales Manager at Motorbooks International Wholesalers & Distributors, Galtier Plaza, Suite 200, 380 Jackson Street, St. Paul, MN 55101-3885, USA.

Library of Congress Cataloguing-in-Publication Data available.

ISBN: 0-7603-1876-X

Produced by:
Amber Books Ltd
Bradley's Close
74–77 White Lion Street
London N1 9PF
www.amberbooks.co.uk

Printed in Singapore

All photographs © 2004 International Masters Publishers AB.

CONTENTS

Introduction

Modifying cars is an art as old as the motor industry itself, with owners of even the very earliest forms of four-wheeled transport choosing to alter their wheels to suit their personal needs. Of course, these early forms of modification were more about practicality than style. Pioneer motorists often converted their cars to carry more people, or turned them into trucks or delivery vans. But they set a precedent that would continue to this day, and changing cars from their manufacturer's intended design to something more personal quickly became an art form.

This book celebrates the works of these car builders. Offering an enthralling look at some of America's most extreme rods and custom cars, it is a tribute to America's impressive, long-lived, and glamorous hot rod and customizing tradition.

Hot rods have been a part of America's automative culture for over seven decades. The custom car can trace its roots back to the birth of mass produced motor cars, and it is no coincidence

that the most popular hot rods were based on Ford's ubiquitious Model T. As car use became more widespread in the United States—around the mid 1920s—second-hand Model Ts dropped in value, as wealthier buyers clamored to get their hands on newer, faster, and more luxurious models. This meant that a lot of Model Ts fell into the hands of young drivers.

The problem was that the Model T had a rather dull and boring image. It may have provided motive power for over 15 million owners, but it was too common, too slow, and too drab to inspire the thrusting young owners that often found themselves in possession of the family's old car. An industry grew up around the popularity of the Model T, one devoted to personalizing it to look a

Hot rodders have taken up the Ford Model T since the 1920s, stripping down the car to make a lightweight racer. The "Bucket T," as shown here, came about in the 1960s as a development of these early stripped-down cars.

little bit different from all the other aged Fords on the road. Streamlined fenders, painted radiators, and chrome accessories became the rage, young drivers saved their cash, and the hot rod was born.

A lack of engine choices and the cost of reengineering a car to take a different powerplant meant that these early hot rods were often crude devices, powered by standard T-Ford engines. Still, rodders found their own ways to make them go faster. Removing non-essential parts of the bodywork, such as the mud guards, roof, and sometimes even the hood, meant that every last ounce of performance could be squeezed out of the T. Early speed merchants like Winfield, Bell, and Cragar appeared, offering engine hop-up parts to further up the performance ante. Some owners even organized illegal street races to see who had built the fastest car. Some Model Ts were stripped down to the absolute bones, leaving little more than a chassis, an engine, and part of the body tub. These were referred to as "Bucket Ts," in reference to the fact that the only remaining bodywork was a "bucket" for the driver to sit in.

RODDERS' REVOLUTION
Wind forward a few years, and the rodders' revolution had become established and the custom car movement was well under way. By the 1950s,

This customized 1950s Ford Crestline Sunliner features many individual touches, including whitewall tires, upmarket hubcaps, grille teeth made from bumper overriders, and a flame paint job to give it that hot rod look.

customized cars were in vogue, and there was a wealth of very different cars available to suit buyers' budgets. The sporty 1930s coupes and roadsters that had cost their owners dear when new were now available for next to nothing, and with a modern V8 under the hood—often salvaged from a wreck in a junkyard—they became a force to be reckoned with on America's boulevards.

By now, two very different types of hot rod owner had emerged. There were the street racers, who now had legal drag strips on which to run. For these guys, styling came second to performance. And although a good-looking car was always popular, performance was their ultimate aim. Modified engines, gearboxes, cylinder heads, and stick-shifters were essential if you wanted to beat the guy in the next lane, while jacked-up suspension allowed the fitting of enormous slick rear tires. A rod of this stripe was never a pleasant machine to drive on the public highway, but in a head-to-head standing quarter mile, grip and straight line performance were much more important than creature comforts.

Away from the drag strip, other rodders were building cars that were more about show than go. Some owners were even taking standard showroom cars and modifying them when they were brand new, with flared fenders, chrome-plated rocker covers, painted bumpers, lowered suspension, magnesium wheels, and hidden door handles. A show paint job was essential, often with a pearlescent or metallic finish and trademark flames down the side.

Although these were two very different types of car builders, the two camps had one thing in common. A love of the automobile, and a desire to create a car that was very much an expression of their individuality.

MUSCLING IN

Even in its early days the custom car culture was changing. By the mid-1960s, America's auto makers, aware that young buyers liked their cars to have power and look hot, were marketing street versions of cars that looked customized. Arguably, General Motors was first to recognize the trend, and in 1964 it offered a souped-up version of the dowdy Pontiac Tempest, targeted at people who would otherwise buy an older model and modify it. The Pontiac GTO was America's primordial muscle car, and the trend it created

undermined the street rod scene. Here were factory-built cars that had all the look of a custom car and all the performance of a drag racer, in an affordable and widely available package.

It was the muscle car era that saw a marked change in the attitudes of America's hot rodders. Guys who enjoyed street racing and standing quarter miles shifted their allegiance away from modified examples of early cars in preference for showroom stock GTOs, Camaros, Chargers, Mustangs, and Firebirds.

But the hot rod was far from dead. In fact, it rose to become bigger than it ever had been before, as a whole industry grew up around those who saw their custom cars as show pieces. Early hot rods, such as Bucket Ts and Ford Coupes, were preserved and held in high esteem as the cars that founded the hot rod revolution, while some rodders opted to modernize the concept, equipping Ford Deuce chassis with modern V8s.

Others created classics of their own, taking the rotten shells of scrapped vintage cars and bringing them back to life as modern-day retro icons, often

The stock 1968 Ford Galaxie was a clean and rather understated design. That look has been totally transformed on this car by a combination of paint, perfect detailing, massive alloy wheels, and painted flames.

equipped with Ford 5.0-liter or Chevy small-block V8 engines; these powerplants were plentiful, easy to get parts for, and easy to tune. These retro-styled cars of the 1930s and 1940s epitomize hot rod ownership. Mention a hot rod to a car enthusiast today, and chances are that he or she will think of something very similar to the Ford Deuce coupes featured in this book.

CUSTOM CLASSICS

Custom cars became classics in their own right, and today there is even a Hot Rod Hall of Fame, located in Afton, Oklahoma, where some of the finest customs in history, built by some of the most famous builders, are preserved for those who worship the custom scene.

But rodders refuse to be stuck in the past. Even some muscle cars came in for hot rod treatment over the years. Give a top customizer any car, and he will turn it into a work of art. The subject does not matter—it is the unique style and the quality of the work that distinguish a proper hot rod from a badly modified stocker.

For that reason, we have chosen a wide variety of subjects within these pages, to give you an insightful look into the minds of the world's hot rodders and custom car builders. Who would have

With more than 400,000 cars built, Volkswagen's sporty Karmann Ghia is a favorite amongst cutomizers. The smooth, sensuous lines of the California look fits this 1960s model perfectly.

ever imagined a hot rod version of a modern Chevrolet Caprice station wagon, for example? Yet you can see it here, and admire how its creator has endowed it with the look of the revered '57 Chevy Nomad, right down to the rear fins and unique salmon-pink paint job.

We have also featured some of the most famous custom cars in history, including those modified by legendary automobile artist Boyd Coddington, the Ford Model B that inspired the Beach Boys to record "Little Deuce Coupe," and the yellow Ford coupe that was the very car featured in the Hollywood blockbuster *American Graffiti*.

Hot rods and custom cars are works of art, and we are sure you will agree that our stunning photographs and breadth of detail encapsulates the sentiment perfectly. Maybe this book will inspire you to create your own custom, or maybe you are just happy to sit back and enjoy this celebration of America's amazingly individual automobile culture. One thing is for sure—every car in these pages is completely unique.

Early HOT RODS

Hot rods have been around for decades and their inception came much, much earlier than most people think. It was way back in the 1940s. The hot rod culture really flourished after World War II—young men had money and wanted to have fast, hot cars.

In the early hot rod scene, the Ford Model B of 1932 was a big influence, as it used the legendary V8 Flathead engine, which could be easily tuned by home mechanics. The hot rodders of the time tuned their cars for speed and raced on the streets, but after this activity became outlawed their hobby developed in a number of different ways.

Hot rodding is a great way to get yourself a unique car that can turn heads and go as fast as much more expensive vehicles.

Salt Lake
Slingshots

As well as racing each other on the streets, hot rodders headed for the biggest open spaces they could find to test their cars' top speeds. The two most notable places include the dry lakes of southern California and the Bonneville Salt Flats of Utah. The salt flats' potential for racing was first recognized in 1896 by W.D. Rishel. He convinced daredevil racer Teddy Tezlaff to attempt an automobile speed record on the flats. Tezlaff drove a Blitzen Benz 141.73 m.p.h. to set an unofficial record in 1914.

Many body styles are still based on early Ford designs, though modern body shapes have also crept into the sport.

Streamlined for speed

Loosely based on a 1926-27 Model T Ford, this rod had streamlined wheels and bodywork, to reduce wind drag and boost the car's top speed. This car set a new record in its class in 1996, travelling at more than 260 mph!

World's fastest rod

Al Teague's streamliner currently holds the wheel-driven land speed record at 393 mph, which he set in 1991.

Jet Power

The raceway on the Bonneville Salt Flats had become the standard course for world land speed records by 1949. Some of the more highly-developed cars have broken land speed records. In the 1960s, jet powered vehicles captured the imagination of the world. In 1970, Gary Gabolich's rocket car, "Blue Flame," achieved a spectacular 622.4 mph. In 1997, Andy Green, a British fighter pilot, driving the jet-powered "Thrust SSC," broke the sound barrier, reaching an incredible 763.035 mph.

UNDER THE SKIN

TYPICAL HOT ROD

A traditional hot rod uses a 1930s Ford coupe and a highly-tuned Ford Flathead engine, or a more modern large-capacity American V8. The rear axle is sometimes made narrower to fit wide rear wheels. Front suspension remains old fashioned, often with the original style of transverse leaf spring still in place but lowered so the car sits closer to the ground.

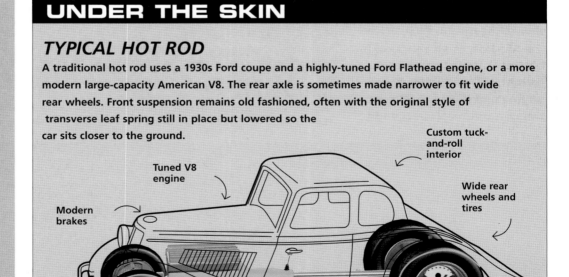

Custom tuck-and-roll interior

Tuned V8 engine

Modern brakes

Wide rear wheels and tires

Lowered front suspension

Narrowed rear axle

Early HOT RODS

A 392 Hemi V8 makes this hot rod accelerate faster than a Porsche Turbo.

Hot rod heaven

There are more hot rods today than there have ever been in the past. Though the types of rods have varied over the years, the basic concept is still there. Hot rods are usually a pre-1954 body, stripped to its bare essentials to reduce its weight, with a highly-tuned engine and have a 0-60 mph time of around five seconds.

Willys

The fat-fendered 1940-41 Willys coupe was another very popular choice for hot rodders and drag racers alike.

Retro rods

Nostalgia-style rods have gained popularity over the past decade. These three Ford Model Ts were built in Essex, England, purely for fun.

Custom coffin

Hot rodders developed the art of customizing. Famous names in that field include George and Sam Barris, the Barris Bros, who hit the big

Accelerative force

Street racing of early hot rods helped develop drag racing. Acceleration was most important here: two cars would pair up at traffic lights and race to the next set of traffic lights for money. This turned into a more precise sport where competitors race each other over a quarter-mile, from a standing start. The first to get to the other end of the 'strip' is the winner.

Dragsters of the 1960s had long bodies and a front-mounted engine that could produce up to 1,000 bhp.

Lead sleds

AND CUSTOMS

Leads sleds often featured custom paint jobs with eye-catching metallic colors and flames. The latter came about as a copy of the guys who fought in World War II and painted flames on the sides of their fighter planes. Pictured here is a typical lead sled— a 1951 Mercury, which is a popular car to turn into a lead sled.

Style over speed

Some hot rodders wanted style more than speed. Body modifications took pride of place, such as roof chops and removing chrome trim. Modifications were smoothed over with lead, sanded, and painted—hence the name 'lead sleds.'

time by making cars for the Munsters series and the Batmobile for the 1960s TV series of Batman. Pictured is 'The Dragula,' Grandpa Munster's creepy car based on a coffin!

LOW-SLUNG LEAD SLEDS

The lead sled is one of the most popular kinds of custom cars. Usually based on late 1940s and early-1950s American cars, modifications are mainly to the bodywork. To give a sleeker profile, suspension is lowered and chopping the top lowers the roofline. Wheel skirts help to heighten the impression. Popular engine choice is a Chevy V8 and remains somewhat stock in performance.

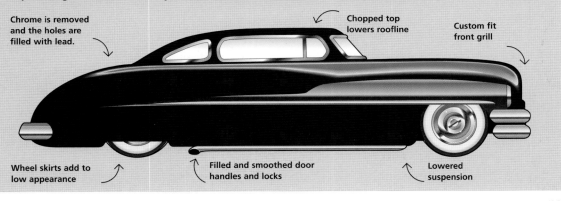

Chrome is removed and the holes are filled with lead.

Chopped top lowers roofline

Custom fit front grill

Wheel skirts add to low appearance

Filled and smoothed door handles and locks

Lowered suspension

Boyd SMOOTHSTER

It may look like a 1937 Ford that was heavily modified but, in fact, the Smoothster is a fabrication exercise where a whole car was created completely from scratch at Boyd Coddington's legendary hot rod shop.

"...one wild ride."

"A lot of attention was paid to the design of the Smoothster's interior. It's surprisingly roomy and the dashboard maximizes the modified feel with a simple three-gauge arrangement. The Corvette-sourced 5.7-liter engine offers ample performance and sends the power to the fat, 18-inch rear tires. The acceleration matches its looks, and stopping is not a problem either since the Smoothster has four-wheel disc brakes. Overall, Boyd's latest creation is one wild ride."

The simple interior reflects the smart and functional philosophy of the Smoothster.

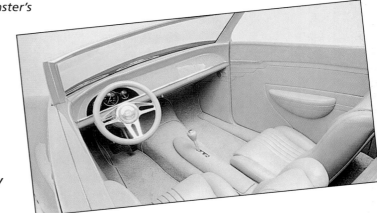

Milestones

1992 Using the body

of a 1937 Ford Convertible, work is started on creating a street-legal hot rod version using a Corvette engine and suspension. A wooden buck is built which is the mold used for the custom aluminum body.

Mid 1930s Fords are among the most popular street rods.

1993 After the original

builder decided not to finish the car, the project is passed on to Hot Rods by Boyd for completion. The electric windows are removed and a removable hardtop replaces the original folding roof.

The Smoothster was based on the 1937 Ford.

1995 Finished in DuPont

'Boyd Yellow' the Smoothster rolls into Oakland's Roadster show. It wins the 'World's Most Beautiful Roadster' award as well as several other first-place trophies.

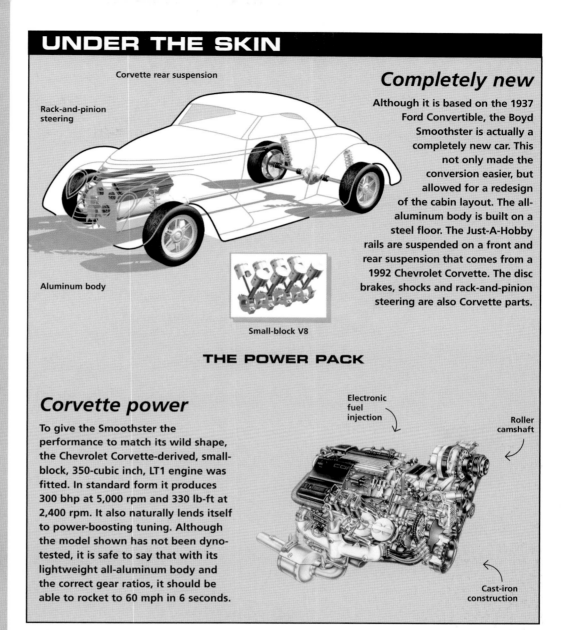

Corvette rear suspension

Rack-and-pinion steering

Aluminum body

Small-block V8

THE POWER PACK

Completely new

Although it is based on the 1937 Ford Convertible, the Boyd Smoothster is actually a completely new car. This not only made the conversion easier, but allowed for a redesign of the cabin layout. The all-aluminum body is built on a steel floor. The Just-A-Hobby rails are suspended on a front and rear suspension that comes from a 1992 Chevrolet Corvette. The disc brakes, shocks and rack-and-pinion steering are also Corvette parts.

Corvette power

To give the Smoothster the performance to match its wild shape, the Chevrolet Corvette-derived, small-block, 350-cubic inch, LT1 engine was fitted. In standard form it produces 300 bhp at 5,000 rpm and 330 lb-ft at 2,400 rpm. It also naturally lends itself to power-boosting tuning. Although the model shown has not been dyno-tested, it is safe to say that with its lightweight all-aluminum body and the correct gear ratios, it should be able to rocket to 60 mph in 6 seconds.

Electronic fuel injection

Roller camshaft

Cast-iron construction

Priceless

The skill and dedication that have gone into producing the Smoothster make it a testimony to what can be achieved if the desire is there. A car such as this is a work of passion, meaning more to its owner than it could to anyone else; for this reason, it's priceless.

Distinctive looks and vivid yellow paint make the Smoothster stand out.

Boyd SMOOTHSTER

It took almost three years and an untold number of man hours to produce the Smoothster. This effort was rewarded in 1995 when it won the 'World's Most Beautiful Roadster' competition in Oakland.

Corvette engine

The 350-cubic inch LT1 engine from a 1992 Corvette was used in the Smoothster because it was a well-proven, reliable unit that fitted the dimensions of the engine bay and produced sufficient power.

Hardtop

Initially, the Smoothster was to have a folding roof. However, Hot Rods by Boyd decided to fit a Carson-style removable hardtop.

Big wheels

Originally, the Smoothster was built to run on 15- and 16-inch wheels. However, Boyd's Wheels developed some new 17- and 18-inch designs, and so the wells were opened up to fit the larger wheels and tires.

Hidden exhausts

To retain its sleek lines, the Smoothster's exhaust pipes are hidden under the running boards.

Art deco grill

The finely ribbed grill consists of 22 hand-formed bars which flow back into the bodywork, with the top rib forming a chrome belt line that runs down the trunk line at the rear.

Aluminum body

The unique aluminum body was formed over a wooden buck. In order to get a smoother appearance, the 1937 Ford has been sectioned, chopped and lowered to produce a fat-fendered look. The floor is made of steel for stiffness and reliability.

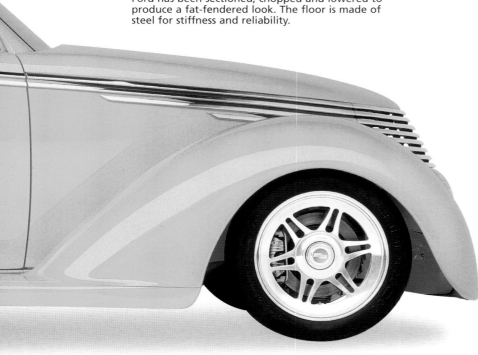

1995 Boyd Smoothster

ENGINE

Type: V8

Construction: Cast-iron block and heads

Valve gear: Two valves per cylinder operated by a single chain-driven camshaft with pushrods

Bore and stroke: 4.00 in. x 3.48 in.

Displacement: 350 c.i.

Compression ratio: 10.25:1

Induction system: Multiport electronic fuel injection

Maximum power: 300 bhp at 5,000 rpm

Maximum torque: 330 lb-ft at 2,400 rpm

Top speed: 122 mph

0-60 mph: 6.0 sec.

TRANSMISSION

Three-speed automatic

BODY/CHASSIS

Aluminum roadster body and steel chassis

SPECIAL FEATURES

The Smoothster retains the 1937 Ford's rear-hinged 'suicide' doors.

Six-spoke tailpipes mimic the design of the alloy wheels.

RUNNING GEAR

Steering: Rack-and-pinion

Front suspension: A-arms with single transverse fiberglass leaf springs, telescopic shock absorbers, and anti-sway bar

Rear suspension: Independent with A-arms transverse fiberglass leaf spring, telescopic shock absorbers, and anti-sway bar

Brakes: Vented discs (front and rear)

Wheels: 16-in. dia. (front), 20-in. dia. (rear)

Tires: 205/45ZR-16 (front), 295/35ZR-18 (rear)

DIMENSIONS

Length: 164.0 in.   **Width:** 78.0 in.

Height: 56.0 in.   **Wheelbase:** 112.0 in.

Track: 63.0 in. (front and rear)

Weight: Not quoted

Buick RIVIERA

Late-1960s Buick Rivieras are not normally associated with the custom scene, but they do have racy styling and big-block power, which lends them well to modifications. The results are often spectacular.

"...V8 offers tremendous go."

"This example has no exterior handles—a remote control solenoid opens the doors and trunk. The Riviera is an easy, comfortable car to drive, helped by the light steering, automatic transmission and very soft ride. Even so, the big 430-cubic inch V8 offers tremendous go, and it can out perform nearly any modern family car. The suspension is surprisingly firm for a late-1960s car, and modern tires give the Riviera substantial grip and cornering ability."

All Rivieras have plush cabins—the seats offer sofa-like levels of comfort.

Milestones

1963 Chasing a growing market for

personal luxury coupes, Buick releases the Riviera. Using a shortened LeSabre™ chassis and engine, it has unique styling by Bill Mitchell. First year sales total 40,000.

From 1971, the Riviera became a much larger car.

1966 The Riviera gets a longer and

wider body with softer contours, and its wheelbase is stretched by 2 inches. The standard engine is now a 425-cubic inch V8 with 340 bhp.

The last rear-wheel drive Riviera incarnation appeared in 1978.

1967 Buick's luxury coupe returns with few

changes but has a new 430-cubic inch engine with 360 bhp. Sales are up to 42,799 this year.

1970 For its final year, the Riviera gets busier

styling with fender skirts, plus a new grill. The 430-cubic inch V8 is enlarged to 455-cubic inches.

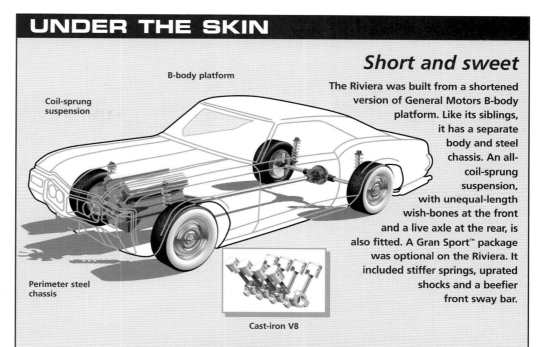

B-body platform

Coil-sprung suspension

Perimeter steel chassis

Cast-iron V8

Short and sweet

The Riviera was built from a shortened version of General Motors B-body platform. Like its siblings, it has a separate body and steel chassis. An all-coil-sprung suspension, with unequal-length wish-bones at the front and a live axle at the rear, is also fitted. A Gran Sport™ package was optional on the Riviera. It included stiffer springs, uprated shocks and a beefier front sway bar.

THE POWER PACK

Tough torquing

Although usually associated with luxury buyers rather than performance-crazed gearheads, Buick nevertheless offered some of the most potent Detroit powerplants in the late 1960s. The 430-cubic inch V8 follows engineering practice of the day in being a cast-iron overhead unit with a single centrally-mounted camshaft. Although larger than the 425 it replaced, it is still rated at 360 bhp in top form but has more torque—475 lb-ft versus 465 lb-ft—and a dual-plane intake manifold.

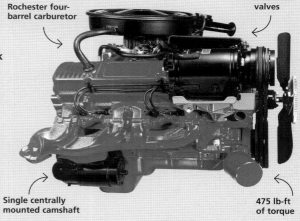

Rochester four-barrel carburetor

Overhead valves

Single centrally mounted camshaft

475 lb-ft of torque

Custom king

Although the 1966-1970 models should not be forgotten, the 1963-1965 Riviera is the favorite. These cars have good build quality, plenty of get-up-and-go, tough mechanicals and many luxury features. They also make a great starting point for customs.

A few well-thought-out individual touches produce a neat Riviera custom.

Buick RIVIERA

Known as 'Phat Riv,' this particular car stands out thanks to its contrasting green paint, white vinyl top and interior. It is also unique in being a custom not normally associated with the street scene.

Big-block V8 engine

With gas selling for around 30 cents a gallon in 1969, a big-block V8 was mandatory in luxury cars like the Riviera. This one has a 430-cubic inch mill with 360 bhp and 475 lb-ft of torque. As expected, this car is exceedingly quick in a straight line.

Custom wheels and tires

No custom is complete without aftermarket wheels and tires. This one has a set of reverse-rim chrome-plated 15-inch steel wheels wearing period-looking modern BFGoodrich whitewall radials.

Smoothed body

A popular custom touch, which is still in vogue, is to smooth the body and remove as much chrome trim as possible. Consequently, this Riviera has had its door handles, trunk latch and trademark side spear chrome trim removed.

Body-on-frame construction

General Motors' larger cars of the 1960s have separate bodies and frames. This saved on production tooling costs, with new bodies being fitted on existing chassis. It also helps in tuning the chassis and suspension for a smooth ride.

Firm setup

The all-coil-sprung suspension is conventional for a car of this type and era, but the Riviera's setup is unusually firm and gives great stability.

Immaculate interior

One feature that really stands out on this car is the interior. The door panels, dashboard and seats have all been upholstered in white leather accentuated by green piping, highlighting the Riviera's luxury status.

Specifications

1969 Buick Riviera

ENGINE

Type: V8

Construction: Cast-iron block and heads

Valve gear: Two valves per cylinder operated by a single camshaft with pushrods and rockers

Bore and stroke: 4.19 in. x 3.90 in.

Displacement: 430 c.i.

Compression ratio: 10.25:1

Induction system: Rochester Quadrajet four-barrel carburetor

Maximum power: 360 bhp at 5,000 rpm

Maximum torque: 475 lb-ft at 3,200 rpm

Top speed: 125 mph

0-60 mph: 7.2 sec.

TRANSMISSION

GM TurboHydramatic three-speed automatic

BODY/CHASSIS

Separate steel chassis with steel two-door coupe body

SPECIAL FEATURES

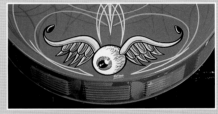

Even the air cleaner has been color-coded to match the exterior.

A popular option on street customs is to french the radio antenna.

RUNNING GEAR

Steering: Recirculating ball

Front suspension: Unequal-length wishbones with coil springs, telescopic shock absorbers and anti-roll bar

Rear suspension: Live axle with coil springs, telescopic shock absorbers and anti-roll bar

Brakes: Discs (front), drums (rear)

Wheels: Steel, 6 x 15 in.

Tires: 175/60 R15

DIMENSIONS

Length: 211.6 in. **Width:** 79.4 in.

Height: 52.7 in. **Wheelbase:** 119.0 in.

Track: 63.5 in. (front), 63.0 in. (rear)

Weight: 4,199 lbs.

Buick T-TYPE

In terms of the world's fastest street car, the McLaren F1 is considered the King of the Hill. However, statistics reveal that this one-of-a-kind Buick T-Type is probably the car most deserving of this prestigious title.

"...something else entirely."

"A street-legal NASCAR racer is perhaps an apt description for this car, but with a passenger seat and a turbocharged V6 under the hood, this Buick is really something else entirely. Start up the engine, floor the throttle and hold on. Before you can blink you will be doing 100 mph, but given a straight road and nerves of steel you can easily push 200 mph. Yet with its competition suspension, brakes and steering, it is a real handler, too."

In a car like this, the two most important instruments are the tach and boost gauge.

Milestones

1982 Buick's Regal
Sport coupe turbo, introduced for 1978, is renamed the T-Type. With performance suspension and blackout trim, it puts out 165 bhp from its 231-cubic inch V6.

The T-Type was Buick's standard factory performance machine from 1984 to 1987.

1984 Power output
on the turbocharged V6 is increased to 200 bhp, thanks to sequential fuel injection.

The meanest of all factory Buick Turbos was the 1987 GNX™.

1986 After a
carryover for 1985, the T-Type gets an air-to-air intercooler for an extra 35 bhp, enabling 0-60 mph acceleration in the high 7-second range.

1987 Basically a
new grill is the only change. Power is now up to 245 bhp, enabling 13.8-second ¼-mile times. Production ends in December.

UNDER THE SKIN

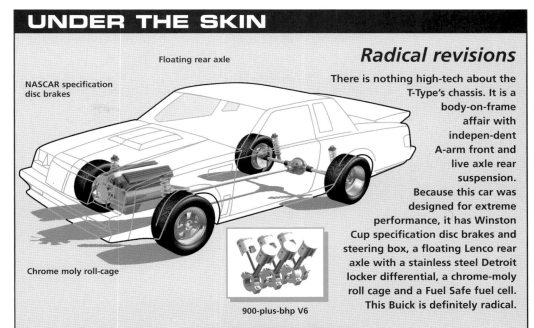

Floating rear axle

NASCAR specification disc brakes

Chrome moly roll-cage

900-plus-bhp V6

Radical revisions

There is nothing high-tech about the T-Type's chassis. It is a body-on-frame affair with indepen-dent A-arm front and live axle rear suspension. Because this car was designed for extreme performance, it has Winston Cup specification disc brakes and steering box, a floating Lenco rear axle with a stainless steel Detroit locker differential, a chrome-moly roll cage and a Fuel Safe fuel cell. This Buick is definitely radical.

THE POWER PACK

Horsepower overkill

Getting 245 bhp from just 3.8 liters in the 1980s was rare. This T-Type, still with a turbo V6, has little in common with the stock piece. It was built by Buick engine master Ken Duttweiler and has Stage II heads with titanium valves, an Edelbrock Victor junior intake (reworked to accept fuel injection plumbing), an Erson roller-lifter camshaft, JE 8.0:1 forged aluminum pistons, MSD injectors, a Ron Davis aluminum radiator, custom-built side tanks and intercooler, plus a dry sump lubrication system. The engine produces from 676 to 967 bhp on a dynamometer with the turbo spooling from 10 and 24 lbs. of boost respectively.

Tuner's dream

Buick built 27,637 T-Types during the car's four-year production run. They were among the quickest cars of the 1980s and very tuner-friendly. With a little work it is possible to get a 9-second ¼ mile ride, and for this reason these cars will always be in demand.

This 967-bhp T-Type started life as a $14,000 sports luxury coupe.

Buick T-TYPE

Built to compete in the Nevada Silver State Challenge, this Buick T-Type, running on 24 lbs. of boost, can go from 0 to 200 mph in 44 seconds— an unbelievable achievement for what started out as a sport luxury coupe.

Monster turbocharged engine

Starting with a 260-cubic inch block, legendary Buick engine builder Ken Duttweiler created a monster of a motor. With Stage II M&A cylinder heads and a massive high performance turbocharger, it has approximately the same output as the GTP racing Turbo V6 engines.

Heavy-duty suspension

As it was designed to carve up corners as well as go ballistic in a straight line, heavy-duty suspension pieces were deemed essential. A Winston Cup specification steering box, a specially designed three-bar link suspension and Carrera shocks help this Buick corner at triple-digit speeds.

Fuel cell

In place of the stock gas tank is a fuel cell built by Fuel Safe. It provides an added safety margin over a standard tank and ensures that there is plenty of gas for the high-volume Mellings fuel pump to feed to the engine.

NASCAR brakes

When a car is capable of over 200 mph, stopping it requires a great deal of effort. Fitting a set of Winston Cup specification rotors and calipers has proved more than adequate.

Specifications

1987 Buick T-Type

ENGINE

Type: V8

Construction: Cast-iron block and alloy aluminum M&A heads

Valve gear: Two valves per cylinder operated by a single V-mounted camshaft with pushrods and rockers

Bore and stroke: Not quoted

Displacement: 260 c.i.

Compression ratio: 8.0:1

Induction system: Sequential electronic fuel injection

Maximum power: 967 bhp at 6,500 rpm

Maximum torque: 877-lb-ft at 5,200 rpm

Top speed: 226 mph

0-60 mph: 2.8 sec.

TRANSMISSION

TH400 three-speed automatic

BODY/CHASSIS

Separate steel chassis with steel and carbon fiber two-door coupe body

SPECIAL FEATURES

An aluminum wing helps increase downforce at high speeds.

Containing wheel tubs and a fuel cell, the trunk has little room for anything else.

RUNNING GEAR

Steering: Recirculating ball

Front suspension: Unequal length A-arms with coil springs, telescopic shock absorbers and anti-roll bar

Rear suspension: Live axle with three-bar links, coil springs, telescopic shock absorbers and anti-roll bar

Brakes: Discs (front and rear)

Wheels: Simmons, 17-in. dia.

Tires: Pirelli P-Zero, 265 x 17 (front), 335 x 17 (rear)

DIMENSIONS

Length: 190.8 in. **Width:** 77.1 in.

Height: 54.9 in. **Wheelbase:** 108.1 in.

Track: 64.5 in. (front), 62.6 in. (rear)

Weight: 3,200 lbs.

Chevrolet **BEL AIR**

Think of America in the 1950s and an image of a 1957 Chevy® will appear, parked outside a period diner. This, the most popular of the so-called classic 'Shoebox-Chevys,' is also a favorite basis for a hot rod.

"...apple pie dynamite."

"This is what American hot-rodding is all about: a classic '57 Chevy® with some serious get-up-and-go. Think of it as apple pie with a stick of dynamite baked right in. Tap the throttle and the whole car rocks with the engine's inertia. Off the line, this car could beat almost any modern production car. Once the huge Mickey Thompson racing rear tires have stopped spinning, the violent acceleration shoves you back into your seat as you hang, white-knuckled, onto the tiny steering wheel."

Flame theme is apparent inside the car, with the graphic appearing on the steering wheel, interior trim and upholstery.

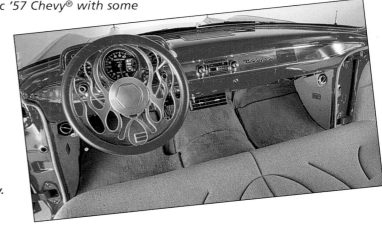

Milestones

1955 Chevrolet releases its new modern line of cars, the 150, 210 and Bel Air series. It is the first sedan to use the new 265-cubic inch V8 small-block engine. Harley Earl's design team matches the engine to well-balanced and modern styling. Its box-styling and clean looks give it the name 'shoebox Chevy.'

The 1957 Bel Air convertible was the top of the line.

1956 The car receives a $40 million restyle for the new model year. Power is boosted on both six- and eight-cylinder models. The top spec V8 with Power-Pak produces 225 bhp.

The 150-series models are identifiable by the 1955-styled side trim.

1957 Another restyle produces the classic 1950s American sedan. The 1957 model uses a larger 283-cubic inch version of the small-block engine with fuel injection for 283 bhp.

1990s By this time, the 1955-57 'shoebox-Chevys' have become true classics in standard and hot-rod forms.

UNDER THE SKIN

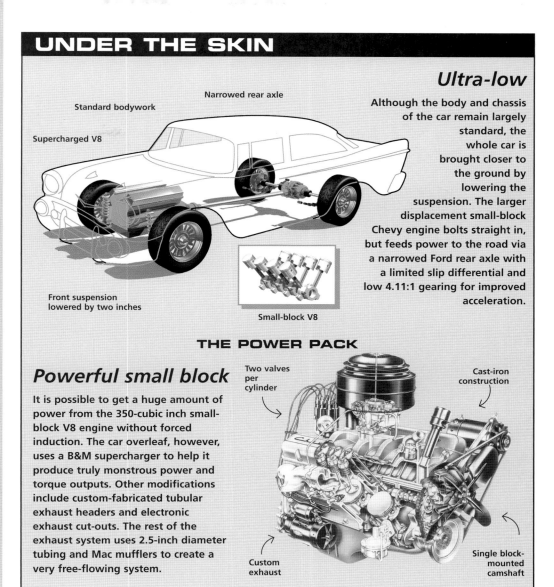

Standard bodywork

Narrowed rear axle

Supercharged V8

Front suspension lowered by two inches

Small-block V8

Ultra-low

Although the body and chassis of the car remain largely standard, the whole car is brought closer to the ground by lowering the suspension. The larger displacement small-block Chevy engine bolts straight in, but feeds power to the road via a narrowed Ford rear axle with a limited slip differential and low 4.11:1 gearing for improved acceleration.

THE POWER PACK

Powerful small block

It is possible to get a huge amount of power from the 350-cubic inch small-block V8 engine without forced induction. The car overleaf, however, uses a B&M supercharger to help it produce truly monstrous power and torque outputs. Other modifications include custom-fabricated tubular exhaust headers and electronic exhaust cut-outs. The rest of the exhaust system uses 2.5-inch diameter tubing and Mac mufflers to create a very free-flowing system.

Two valves per cylinder

Cast-iron construction

Custom exhaust

Single block-mounted camshaft

Boyd's best

Master hot-rod builder Boyd Coddington created the Boydair as a showcase for his hot-rod building company. It has a custom-made chassis clothed in modified 1957 Chevy panels. It's centered around the cowl and windshield of a 1959 Chevrolet Impala®. The engine and running gear are from a 1997 Corvette®.

Ultra-low 'Boydair' uses modern Corvette mechanicals.

Chevrolet BEL AIR

Huge tires, an immaculate custom paint job, a wild interior, low aggressive stance and a powerful blown V8 engine installed in a classic American car—all the ingredients of a great hot rod.

Chromework

Although this car has been built as a high-performance vehicle, little has been done to reduce its weight. Even the heavy chrome bumpers are retained.

Blown engine

A B&M supercharger gives a huge boost to the power and torque outputs of this car's 350-cubic inch small-block Chevy V8 engine.

Custom interior

It looks just as good inside. The flame motif is carried through to the interior and even appears on the headlining and steering wheel.

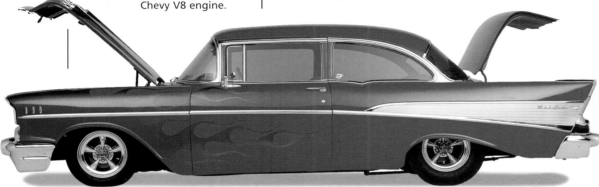

Alloy wheels

The popular American Racing Torq-Thrust five-spoke wheels are used. They are similar in style to racing wheels often used in the 1960s.

Lowered suspension

To lower the lines of the car and give it that road-hugging stance, the suspension has been lowered. Two-inch drop spindles and chopped coil springs lower the front, while custom semi-elliptic leaf springs, relocated on the chassis, ease down the rear end.

Huge rear tires

The Mickey Thompson tires added to the rear of the car are designed to give maximum traction off the line.

Smoothed hood and trunk

Both the hood and rear deck have been smoothed off and stripped of badges to give the car a much cleaner look.

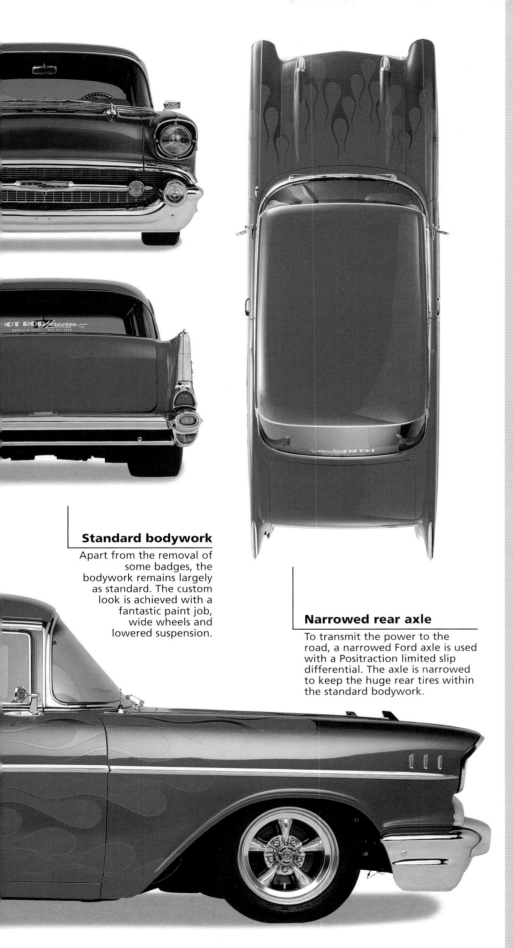

Standard bodywork

Apart from the removal of some badges, the bodywork remains largely as standard. The custom look is achieved with a fantastic paint job, wide wheels and lowered suspension.

Narrowed rear axle

To transmit the power to the road, a narrowed Ford axle is used with a Positraction limited slip differential. The axle is narrowed to keep the huge rear tires within the standard bodywork.

Specifications
1957 Modified Chevrolet Bel Air

ENGINE

Type: V8
Construction: Cast-iron block and heads
Valve gear: Single block-mounted camshaft operating two valves per cylinder via pushrods
Bore and stroke: 4 in. x 3.5 in.
Displacement: 350 c.i.
Compression ratio: 8.5:1
Induction system: B&M 4-71 mechanical supercharger with Holley four-barrel carb
Maximum power: 420 bhp at 5,400 rpm
Maximum torque: 435 lb-ft at 2,500 rpm
Top speed: 147 mph
0-60 mph: 3.9 sec.

TRANSMISSION

350 Turbo automatic

BODY/CHASSIS

Standard 1957 Bel Air steel body with smoothed hood and rear deck on steel perimeter chassis

SPECIAL FEATURES

Above: To achieve its enormous power output, the hot 350-cubic inch V8 uses a B&M supercharger.
Left: This car features outstanding chromework. The hidden gas filler cap is a typical feature for a car of the '50s.

RUNNING GEAR

Steering: Power-assisted recirculating ball
Front suspension: Fabricated tubular wishbones, 2-in. drop spindles, chopped coil springs, telescopic shock absorbers
Rear suspension: Custom semi-elliptic leaf springs, lowering blocks, traction bars and air shock absorbers
Brakes: Discs (front and rear)
Wheels: American Racing Torq-Thrust D, 7.5 in. x 15 in. (front), 11 in. x 15 in. (rear)
Tires: BF Goodrich 205/60-15 (front), Mickey Thompson Sportsman I N50/15 (rear)

DIMENSIONS

Length: 200 in.   **Width:** 73.9 in.
Height: 46.9 in.   **Wheelbase:** 115 in.
Track: 58 in. (front), 58.8 in. (rear)
Weight: 3,197 lbs.

Chevrolet **CAPRICE**

The big Caprice station wagon has a look that endears it to customizers. Possibly the most radical alteration to this example is the 1957 retro styling that includes vintage Nomad® rear quarter panels, chrome trim and hood bullets.

"...incredible presence."

"By any standards a late model Caprice is big. If you want razor-sharp handling, you'd better look elsewhere, but if you dig cruising, the Caprice is hard to fault. Its torquey V8 and four-speed automatic provide smooth power delivery and the will to climb even the steepest grades. With its factory LTZ package and lowered suspension, cornering limits are higher than you'd expect, but, more importantly, this Caprice has incredible presence on the street."

Its interior has all the amenities including a billet steering wheel and custom upholstery.

Milestones

1990 A restyled Caprice goes on sale in April for the 1991 model year.

1991 A larger 5.7-liter engine joins the standard 170-bhp, 5.0-liter unit.

One of the most modified Caprices is actor Tim Allen's Binford LT-5-powered Impala SS.

1993 In response to flagging sales, the Caprice gets a mild facelift with larger rear wheel cut-outs and a revised taillight panel. Station wagons retain unradiused rear wheel wells.

The Chevrolet Caprice puts in its final appearance for 1996.

1994 The Caprice gets the 260-bhp LT1 engine as an option, and a new 4.3-liter V8 replaces the old 305 unit as the base engine. A sporty Impala SS™ makes its debut.

1996 GM drops its big B-body cars and production stops at the Arlington, Texas, plant in favor of full-size trucks.

UNDER THE SKIN

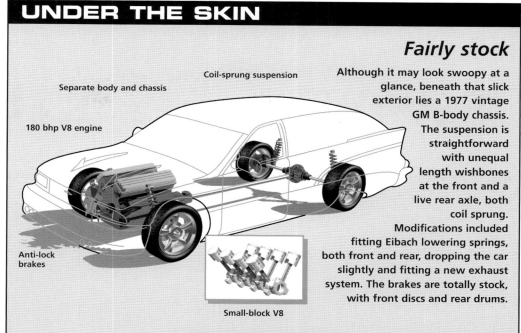

Separate body and chassis

Coil-sprung suspension

180 bhp V8 engine

Anti-lock brakes

Small-block V8

Fairly stock

Although it may look swoopy at a glance, beneath that slick exterior lies a 1977 vintage GM B-body chassis. The suspension is straightforward with unequal length wishbones at the front and a live rear axle, both coil sprung. Modifications included fitting Eibach lowering springs, both front and rear, dropping the car slightly and fitting a new exhaust system. The brakes are totally stock, with front discs and rear drums.

THE POWER PACK

Old reliable

By 1992, the Caprice had become exclusively V8 powered. The base engine was a 170-bhp, 305-cubic inch V8, but a larger 350-cubic inch (5.7-liter) unit was optional. An overhead valve, cast-iron pushrod engine, it dates back to the veteran Chevy small-block unit of 1955. Equipped with throttle-body fuel injection, it puts out 180 bhp in stock tune, but torque is where it really shines with 300 lb-ft at a low 2,400 rpm. This makes it perfect for hauling heavy loads and towing trailers.

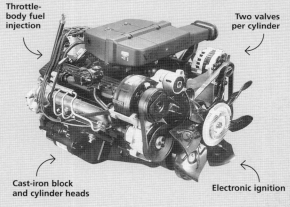

Throttle-body fuel injection

Two valves per cylinder

Cast-iron block and cylinder heads

Electronic ignition

Later models

The best choice for a custom is one of the later wagons, with the 260-bhp LT1 engine and the LTZ package. In stock trim, these cars can rocket to 60 mph in about 8 seconds, plus they are cheap to service with a large supply of parts available.

Late-model Caprice wagons have gained interest from customizers.

Chevrolet CAPRICE

With its massive size and torquey V8, the late model Caprice wagon is almost a natural for custom crafting. This one blends modern aero styling with the classic look of a 1957 Nomad almost to perfection.

V8 engine
With so much bulk, only a V8 is sufficient to power this Caprice. Sitting between the fenderwells is a 350-cubic inch (5.7-liter) overhead valve pushrod engine. It puts out 180 bhp and a substantial amount (300 lb-ft) of torque.

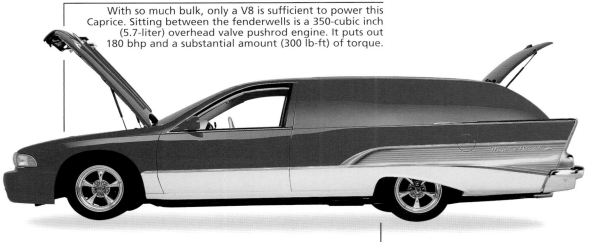

Classic wheels
Many modern street machines feature wide-spoke alloy wheels, either machined from billet steel or cast-aluminum. In keeping with the retro theme however, this Caprice 'Alternomad' has a set of classic-style American Racing Torque Thrust wheels.

Trick body modifications
To achieve retromobile status, the stock Caprice rear fenders have been removed and replaced with reproduction 1957 Nomad items. The roof rack, door and trunk handles and locks have also been removed.

Traditional engineering

Beneath the fantastically styled body lies a 1977 vintage separate chassis. This Caprice came from the factory with a handling suspension, but has been lowered by 1 inch.

Interior alterations

The whole interior has been finished in two-tone red and white, which adds a touch of class. Unique features include rearward facing back seats and the word 'Nomad' embroidered in the rear inside quarter panels.

Front end treatment

On this car, an Impala SS style grill and a new front valance with integral driving lights and air dam have been added, resulting in a sporty look.

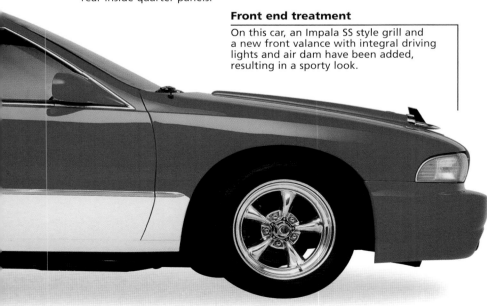

Specifications
1992 Chevrolet Caprice Wagon

ENGINE

Type: V8

Construction: Cast-iron block and heads

Valve gear: Two valves per cylinder operated by pushrods and rockers

Bore and stroke: 4.00 in. x 3.48 in.

Displacement: 350 c.i.

Compression ratio: 8.6:1

Induction system: Throttle-body fuel injection

Maximum power: 180 bhp at 4,000 rpm

Maximum torque: 300 lb-ft at 2,400 rpm

Top speed: 120 mph

0-60 mph: 9.8 sec.

TRANSMISSION

GM 700R4 four-speed automatic

BODY/CHASSIS

Steel station wagon body on separate steel chassis

SPECIAL FEATURES

These twin chromed rockets mimic the hood treatment of a 1957 Chevrolet.

Torque Thrust wheels add a retro touch to this wagon.

RUNNING GEAR

Steering: Recirculating ball

Front suspension: Unequal length wishbones with coil springs, telescopic shock absorbers and anti-roll bar

Rear suspension: Live axle with telescopic shock absorbers and anti-roll bar

Brakes: Discs (front), drums (rear)

Wheels: American Racing Torque Thrust II, 7 x 16 in.

Tires: P275/50 ZR16

DIMENSIONS

Length: 205.0 in.

Width: 71.8 in.

Height: 57.1 in.

Wheelbase: 116.0 in.

Track: 65.9 in. (front), 63.9 in. (rear)

Weight: 4,120 lbs.

Chevrolet CORVETTE

As one of the U.S.'s few sports cars, the Corvette has been desirable since the day it first rolled of the assembly line in 1953. Although fast in stock trim, some people just cannot resist the urge to make these cars even more powerful.

"...A 409-powered Corvette?"

"A 409-powered Corvette? It is a fact that no such production car was built, but then, this is not your run-of-the-mill sports car. There are few creature comforts inside, but once on the move, this ceases to matter. The classic Chevy V8 gives plenty of power right through the rev range, and six speeds enable you to get the most from it. Turn-in is sharp thanks to the steering, and a low center of gravity results in race car-type handling."

Cream leather seats are the only concession to luxury in the functional interior.

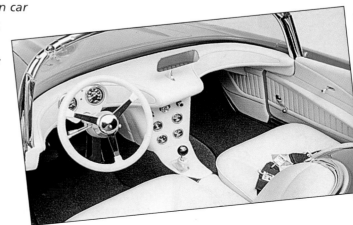

Milestones

1958 The Corvette is heavily
facelifted, with chrome accents on the coves and trunk, plus quad headlights, vents on the hood and revised wheel covers. In this recession year, production jumps from 6,339 to 9,168. The base 283 gets an extra 10 bhp while the fuelie version makes up to 290.

The Corvette entered production in 1953. They were all painted white and had red interiors.

1959 Minor changes,
including the elimination of the trunk straps and hood vents conspire to give a cleaner appearance. Power ratings remain unchanged, but sales near the 10,000 mark.

The 1963 Sting Ray® marked a new direction for the Corvette.

1961 New rear styling,
inspired by the 1957 Sting Ray racer, mates well with the front-end design. The grill is changed to a mesh pattern and the headlight bezels are painted instead of chrome. The fuelie V8 is up to 315 bhp.

UNDER THE SKIN

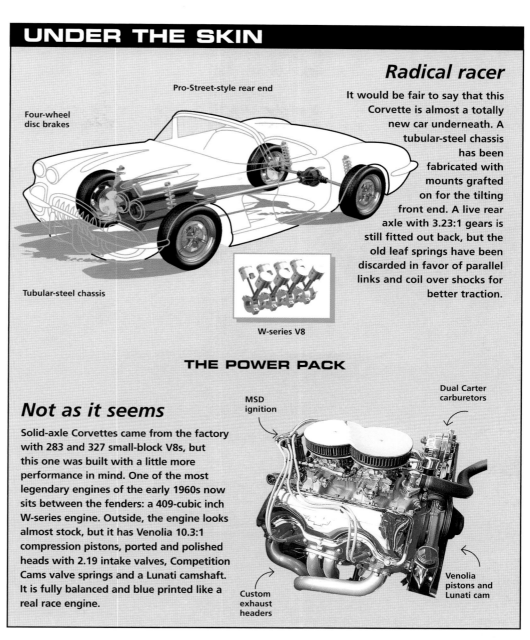

Four-wheel disc brakes

Pro-Street-style rear end

Tubular-steel chassis

W-series V8

Radical racer

It would be fair to say that this Corvette is almost a totally new car underneath. A tubular-steel chassis has been fabricated with mounts grafted on for the tilting front end. A live rear axle with 3.23:1 gears is still fitted out back, but the old leaf springs have been discarded in favor of parallel links and coil over shocks for better traction.

THE POWER PACK

Not as it seems

Solid-axle Corvettes came from the factory with 283 and 327 small-block V8s, but this one was built with a little more performance in mind. One of the most legendary engines of the early 1960s now sits between the fenders: a 409-cubic inch W-series engine. Outside, the engine looks almost stock, but it has Venolia 10.3:1 compression pistons, ported and polished heads with 2.19 intake valves, Competition Cams valve springs and a Lunati camshaft. It is fully balanced and blue printed like a real race engine.

MSD ignition

Dual Carter carburetors

Custom exhaust headers

Venolia pistons and Lunati cam

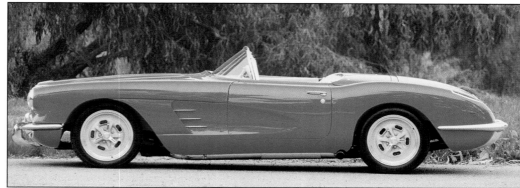

Solid axle

Somewhat overshadowed by the Sting Ray, the 1958-1962 Corvettes still have strong collector interest and are among the most popular Corvettes with the custom fraternity. They are fairly rare and considerably expensive, but the end result is often worth it.

Pre-1963 Corvettes are nicknamed 'solid axles' because of their live rear axle.

Chevrolet CORVETTE

Few cars can capture the spirit of the late 1950s as well as the Corvette. This tasteful though radically modified example does a lot more than capture spirits—it captures show trophies, too.

Performance engine

The Beach Boys sang its praise, justifiably, considering the 409 was one of the most potent hi-po V8s of the early 1960s. Although expensive to build and not easy to modify, experienced engine builders are able to coax tremendous power from it.

Fiberglass body

Since its introduction in 1953, the Corvette has always had fiberglass bodywork. This was decided late in the development stage, as it would prove more cost effective than steel and Kirksite—which was originally intended.

Lowered suspension

By dropping the front and rear ends, the center of gravity is lowered, which, combined with the gas shocks and Goodyear GSC tires results in one of the sharpest-handling Corvettes around.

Spartan interior

Everything about this car screams performance and function. The interior may be draped in cream colored leather, but there is no convertible roof, air conditioning or stereo. However, a full set of Stewart-Warner gauges keeps the driver fully informed.

Cleaned-up body

The 1958 Vette has more glitz than its predecessors, but this was only in keeping with buyer tastes of the time. This one looks positively demure, with its monochromatic Rally Orange paint and absence of chrome accents on the door coves.

Tubular chassis

A completely custom-fabricated chassis lies beneath the bodywork, though thanks to considerable ingenuity, the stock front suspension has been mated to it.

Small windshield

It may look cut down, but the windshield is actually the stock full-length piece, just lowered four inches into the cowl.

Stock hood

Even though the whole front end can be tilted forward, the hood can still open independently for routine maintenance and tuning so essential for hot rods.

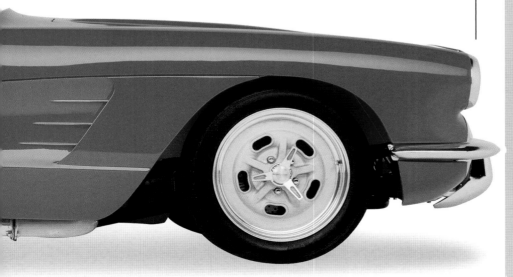

Specifications

1959 Chevrolet Corvette

ENGINE

Type: V8

Construction: Cast-iron block and heads

Valve gear: Two valves per cylinder operated by pushrods and rockers

Bore and stroke: 4.31 x 3.50 in.

Displacement: 416 c.i.

Compression ratio: 10.3:1

Induction system: Dual Carter AFB four-barrel carburetors

Maximum power: 454 bhp at 5,500 rpm

Maximum torque: 460 lb-ft at 5,500 rpm

Top speed: 164 mph

0-60 mph: 4.6 sec.

TRANSMISSION

Richmond six-speed manual

BODY/CHASSIS

Tubular-steel chassis with fiberglass convertible body

SPECIAL FEATURES

The whole front end tilts forward for access to the engine.

Auxiliary gauges are neatly housed in the center console, which is color-keyed with the rest of the interior.

RUNNING GEAR

Steering: Worm-and-ball

Front suspension: Unequal-length A-arms with coil springs, telescopic shock absorbers and sway bar

Rear suspension: Live axle with upper and lower parallel links, coil springs and telescopic shock absorbers

Brakes: Discs, (front and rear)

Wheels: Slotted Magnesium 15.0-in. dia.

Tires: Goodyear Eagle GS-C

DIMENSIONS

Length: 177.2 in.   **Width:** 70.5 in.

Height: 48.2 in.   **Wheelbase:** 102.0 in.

Track: 56.2 in. (front), 55.6 in. (rear)

Weight: 2,620 lbs.

Chevrolet COUPE

If you were after a sporty Chevrolet in 1940, you bought a Coupe. Those old customers would have been shocked if they discovered it had the 125 mph performance like this one, with vast V8 power they could only have dreamt about.

"Fangio's winner."

"The Coupe was good enough for world champion driver Fangio to win an epic 6,000-mile marathon in 1940. Imagine how quick he'd have been in this one. The extra 215 bhp comes from a Corvette™ V8 and a new suspension all around, along with big sticky tires, makes it grip like Fangio could never imagine. Modern Corvette seats replace the high chairs of the original and hold you in place as the Coupe corners with g-forces Fangio never experienced. It'll rocket to 60 mph in under seven seconds and has a top speed of 125 mph."

Corvette leather seats, matching leather trim and a custom alloy-paneled dashboard complete the hot rod touch.

Milestones

1933 Chevy launches
the new Master Eagle model line. It isn't Chevy's first six-cylinder, but its performance and style make it a huge seller.

1937 Redesign for the
Master series makes it even more popular. From 1934 you can have independent front suspension on the Master Deluxe series.

The 1940 Chevy Coupe was quite a fast vehicle in its day.

1940 Longer
wheelbase and restyling set the 1940 series apart. The year also marks the first use of some plastic parts and stainless-steel trim. Driving a Coupe version of the Chevrolet Master, Juan Manuel Fangio wins the 6,000-mile Gran Premio International del Norte race in South America by over an hour, averaging over 55 mph.

1941 214-cubic inch
six gets another 5 bhp, taking it up to 90 bhp, to celebrate new longer, lower and wider bodies mounted on a longer wheelbase.

1942 All car
production, Chevrolet included, comes to an end as factories turn to war production.

UNDER THE SKIN

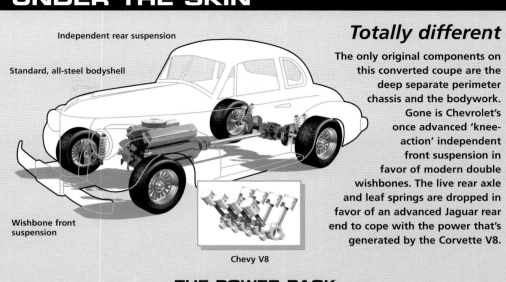

Independent rear suspension

Standard, all-steel bodyshell

Wishbone front suspension

Chevy V8

Totally different

The only original components on this converted coupe are the deep separate perimeter chassis and the bodywork. Gone is Chevrolet's once advanced 'knee-action' independent front suspension in favor of modern double wishbones. The live rear axle and leaf springs are dropped in favor of an advanced Jaguar rear end to cope with the power that's generated by the Corvette V8.

THE POWER PACK

Three times the power

Where it once had an 85-bhp six, the Coupe now has a 327-cubic inch V8. The familiar small-block Chevy® had not even been thought of when the Coupe was being built, but the all-iron pushrod V8 is small enough to drop in the engine bay with ease. As an extra bonus, it's lighter than the engine it replaced. Here it's been dressed up with custom-made tubular headers to make a free-flow exhaust that liberates some extra power. The carbs changed to a trio of twin-choke Rochesters rather than the single four-barrel normally used.

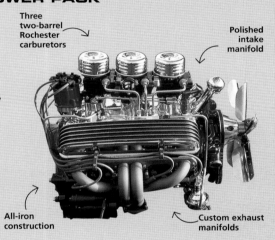

Three two-barrel Rochester carburetors

Polished intake manifold

All-iron construction

Custom exhaust manifolds

Cute rear end

What made the Coupe stand out was the rear end design. From the front doors back, the standard clumsy upright (but more spacious) sedan lines were replaced with tiny rear windows and long flowing rear fenders on either side of a big curved trunk. It wasted passenger space but, as Chevrolet said, it certainly "had enhanced eye appeal" and gave room for plenty of luggage.

Long sloping rear end made the Coupe look better than the sedan.

Chevrolet COUPE

If the small-block Chevy V8 had been around in 1940, Chevrolet would surely have installed it in the Coupe. But would they have been generous enough to give it 300 bhp and Jaguar independent rear suspension? No way—you have to do that yourself.

Custom interior
A custom interior complements the late-model Corvette leather seats. In contrast, it has a classic steering wheel with sprung spokes.

Corvette V8
When this Business Coupe was built, it had Chevrolet's excellent 214-cubic inch straight-six engine with overhead valves, cast-iron block, heads and pistons, a low (6.5:1) compression ratio and a modest 85 bhp at 3,200 rpm. Now it's got a 327-cubic inch Corvette engine with as much as 300 bhp.

Rack-and-pinion steering
Recirculating ball steering was adequate for the Business Coupe, but with 300 bhp at its disposal, it needs a more precise steering system—the rack and pinion is from a European Ford.

Jaguar rear suspension
The Coupe's live rear axle with its semi-elliptic leaf springs has been replaced by the advanced all-independent system from a Jaguar XJ6. Because the Jaguar is much wider than the old Chevy, the suspension had to be narrowed to fit.

Vented disc brakes

The hydraulic drums of the original car were good in their day, but would be light years away from the stopping power of its current brakes. Vented discs at the front are gripped by the same four-piston calipers used on Triumph's old TR8 sports car.

Inboard rear brakes

Because it's now equipped with the complete Jaguar rear suspension unit, this Business Coupe has inboard rear disc brakes.

Larger rear wheels and tires

To help give the Coupe its aggressive nose-down look, 15-inch wheels are used at the back and 14-inch rims up front. Its tires are also wildly different.

Specifications
1940 Modified Chevrolet Coupe

ENGINE

Type: Chevrolet Corvette V8
Construction: Cast-iron block and heads
Valve gear: Two valves per cylinder operated by single block-mounted camshaft via pushrods, rockers and hydraulic lifters
Bore and stroke: 4 in. x 3.24 in.
Displacement: 327 c.i.
Compression ratio: 10.5:1
Induction system: Three two-barrel Rochester carburetors
Maximum power: 300 bhp at 5,000 rpm
Maximum torque: 321 lb-ft at 3,200 rpm
Top speed: 125 mph
0-60 mph: 6.8 sec.

TRANSMISSION

Four-speed automatic

BODY/CHASSIS

Box section perimeter chassis with steel two-door coupe body

SPECIAL FEATURES

Although the hood has been cleared of most ornamentation, the mascot has been left on.

A top quality paint job and super-shiny chromework are a must on a rod.

RUNNING GEAR

Steering: Rack-and-pinion
Front suspension: Double wishbones with coil springs and telescopic shocks
Rear suspension: Modified Jaguar XJ6 rear suspension with wishbones, four coil springs and telescopic shocks
Brakes: Ford vented discs with four-piston calipers front, Jaguar inboard discs rear
Wheels: Alloy Torq-Thrust, 14 in. dia. (front), 15 in. dia. (rear)
Tires: Bridgestone 185/70 14 (front), BF Goodrich 255/70 15 (rear)

DIMENSIONS

Length: 190.2 in. **Width:** 70 in.
Height: 68 in. **Wheelbase:** 112.2 in.
Track: 57.5 in. (front), 59 in. (rear)
Weight: 2,900 lbs.

Chevrolet FLEETMASTER

Early postwar Chevrolets were solid, dependable cars, but comfort and finesse were overlooked. Their bulbous, slab-sided bodies and simple engineering, however, make these models very popular among street rodders.

"...smooth and satisfying."

"While postwar, fat-bodied Chevrolets aren't usually a customizer's first choice, they do make a striking street machine. An inviting interior and comfortable seats make this Chevy® an ideal summertime tourer. Plus, with 325 bhp from a mildly massaged 350 and an automatic trans-mission, satisfying performance is always on tap. With a better suspension, including a Mustang-II rack-and-pinion and a Ford 9-inch rear, this Chevy handles better than it did in stock guise."

A modern leather bench seat contrasts with the vintage instrument panel.

Milestones

1945 Like most Detroit
manufacturers, Chevy resumes civilian production, fielding warmed-over 1942 cars as 1946 models. Although outpaced by rival Ford, the division still manages to churn out 398,026 cars.

A Chevy Fleetmaster was used to pace the 1948 Indy 500.

1947 Apart from a new grill
and equipment changes, the Chevy lineup differs little from the previous year. Models are divided into Style-master®, Fleetmaster and Fleet-line®, the same since 1942. A 90 bhp, 216-cubic inch Stovebolt Six is standard across the board.

The hottest of the Stovebolt Six engines was the 'Blue Flame Special, found in the Corvette.

1948 Although its lineup
changes very little, Chevrolet now outpaces Ford in the production stakes building a staggering 696,449 cars. An all-new Chevy debuts for 1949.

UNDER THE SKIN

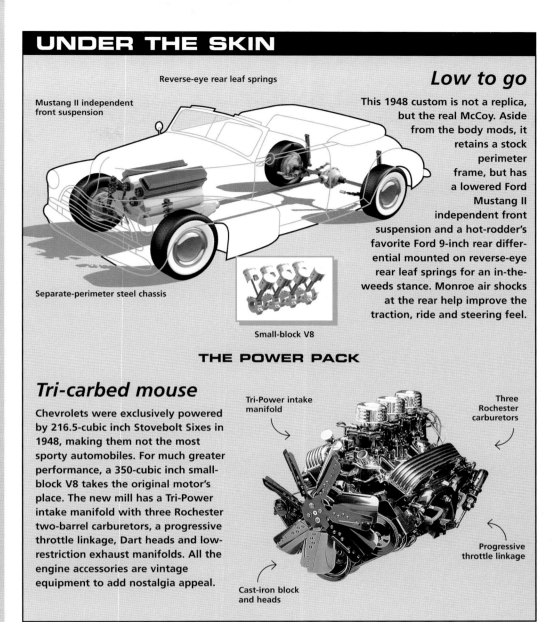

Reverse-eye rear leaf springs

Mustang II independent front suspension

Separate-perimeter steel chassis

Small-block V8

Low to go

This 1948 custom is not a replica, but the real McCoy. Aside from the body mods, it retains a stock perimeter frame, but has a lowered Ford Mustang II independent front suspension and a hot-rodder's favorite Ford 9-inch rear differential mounted on reverse-eye rear leaf springs for an in-the-weeds stance. Monroe air shocks at the rear help improve the traction, ride and steering feel.

THE POWER PACK

Tri-carbed mouse

Chevrolets were exclusively powered by 216.5-cubic inch Stovebolt Sixes in 1948, making them not the most sporty automobiles. For much greater performance, a 350-cubic inch small-block V8 takes the original motor's place. The new mill has a Tri-Power intake manifold with three Rochester two-barrel carburetors, a progressive throttle linkage, Dart heads and low-restriction exhaust manifolds. All the engine accessories are vintage equipment to add nostalgia appeal.

Tri-Power intake manifold

Three Rochester carburetors

Progressive throttle linkage

Cast-iron block and heads

Heavy Chevy

Big and chubby, the early postwar Chevys are not ideal for drag racing, but they do have great potential for lead sleds or customs. The convertibles especially, with chopped, channeled and smoothed bodies give new meaning to the term 'street machine.'

Smoothed and chopped, the 1948 Chevy takes on a whole new look.

Chevrolet FLEETMASTER

Subtle but extremely well-detailed with a luxurious interior and sound yet simple mechanicals, this 1948 Chevy shows that old cars can be turned into immensely practical yet stylish drivers.

Tri-powered 350 V8

Multi-carb setups were one of the most straightforward routes to gaining more horsepower in the 1950s and 1960s. In keeping with its period image, this 1948 Chevy has a classic trio of two-barrel Rochesters.

Mustang II front suspension

Lurking under the front fenders is the street rodder's favorite front clip—a Mustang II independent front suspension. The spindles have been dropped 2½ inches. This serves to improve handling and accentuate the bulging front-end styling.

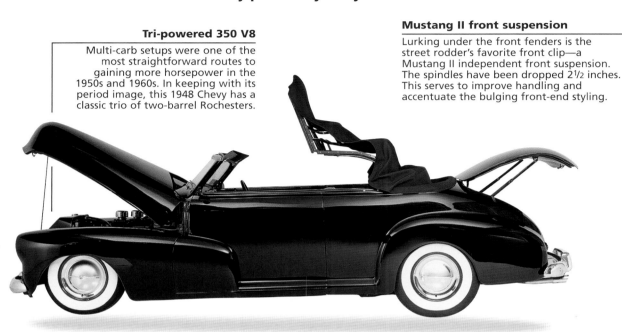

Chopped and channeled body

With their round fenders and bulbous stance, it seems only natural to exaggerate the contours of 1942-1948 Chevys. This stock OEM body has been chopped 3½ inches and smoothed, plus the fenders and hood have been reshaped to match the contours for a look appropriate to the car's name— 48 Chubby.

Period piece

The whole shape of the car was done as a finished example of what original GM design sketches might have resulted in back in the 1940s, unencumbered by cost or manufacturing restrictions.

Bulletproof rear end

A Ford 9–inch rear end, packing streetwise 3.25:1 cogs replaces the stock rear. The axle is mounted on reverse-eye leaf springs to lower the ride height.

Specifications

1948 Chevrolet Fleetmaster

ENGINE

Type: V8

Construction: Cast-iron block and heads

Valve gear: Two valves per cylinder operated by a single, V-mounted camshaft with pushrods and rockers

Bore and stroke: 4.00 in. x 3.48 in.

Displacement: 350 c.i.

Compression ratio: N/A

Induction system: Three Rochester two-barrel carburetors

Maximum power: 325 bhp at 5,500 rpm

Maximum torque: 340 lb-ft at 3,500 rpm

Top speed: 139 mph

0-60 mph: 6.8 sec.

TRANSMISSION

GM TH400 three-speed automatic

BODY/CHASSIS

Perimeter steel chassis with separate two-door convertible body

SPECIAL FEATURES

A vacuum-controlled flap at the base of the windshield feeds cooler, denser air to the carburetors.

Both the front and rear bench seats have been neatly upholstered in soft, modern leather.

RUNNING GEAR

Steering: Rack-and-pinion

Front suspension: Short/long arms with coil springs, telescopic shock absorbers and anti-roll bar

Rear suspension: Live axle, semi-elliptic leaf springs and telescopic shock absorbers

Brakes: Discs (front), drums (rear)

Wheels: Stamped steel, 15-in. dia.

Tires: Kelley Springfield, 215 x 15 in. (front), 235 x 15 in. (rear)

DIMENSIONS

Length: 183.7 in. **Width:** 72.5 in.

Height: 58.1 in. **Wheelbase:** 116.0 in.

Track: 53.5 in. (front and rear)

Weight: 3,450 lbs.

Chevrolet **IMPALA**

One of the most popular cars to turn into a low rider is the Chevrolet Impala. It's not built for all-out power, nor does it handle like a fine Italian sports car. Lowriders were simply made to cruise with class.

"...built to turn heads"

"Despite its long and low appearance, this beautiful Impala drives pretty much as it did when it left the factory in 1959. The 315-bhp engine really makes the heavy car move at indecent speeds when you put your foot down. But it has been built to turn heads, not to break the land speed record. Its ground-hugging stance means that it can bottom-out on really rough surfaces, and so it's best to sit back, take it easy and cruise."

Wide bench seats allow the Impala to carry up to six people in total comfort.

Milestones

1958 Chevrolet
introduces the Impala name, as the top model in the Bel Air line. The 348-cubic inch big-block V8 is launched.

The earlier 1955-1957 shoebox-Chevys had much more rounded styling. This is a 1957 Nomad.

1959 The Impala
becomes a model in its own right. Despite somewhat wild styling, it is well received by the motoring press. There are three body styles: a four-door sedan, a two-door coupe, and a convertible coupe.

The new-for-1959 El Camino™ pick-up had a great deal in common with the Impala.

1960 A subtle
restyle is undertaken for the 1960 model range. The new car has a more conventional front end without the previous year's headlight 'eyebrows'. The distinctive 'cat's eye' tail lights are replaced by a trio of more conventional round lights. The top-spec 348-cubic inch engine now produce 315 bhp.

UNDER THE SKIN

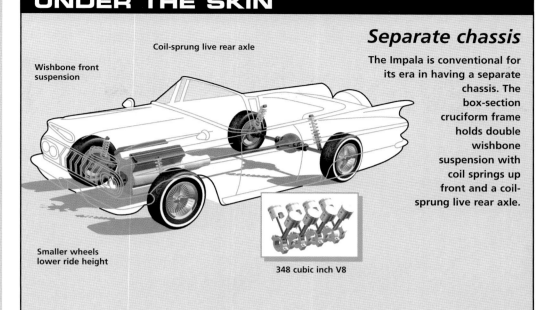

Wishbone front suspension

Coil-sprung live rear axle

Smaller wheels lower ride height

348 cubic inch V8

Separate chassis

The Impala is conventional for its era in having a separate chassis. The box-section cruciform frame holds double wishbone suspension with coil springs up front and a coil-sprung live rear axle.

THE POWER PACK

Stock big block

The 1959 Impala was offered with a choice of engines, from a 236 cubic inch straight-six producing 135 bhp, right up to a 315-bhp, 348 cubic inch V8. The V8 was typical for the time, being a simple design with a single central camshaft operating two valves per cylinder via pushrods and rockers. Top-spec V8s had three two-barrel Rochester carburetors, while the less powerful engines made do with a single four-barrel unit. This car has a stock V8 with three two-barrel carburetors.

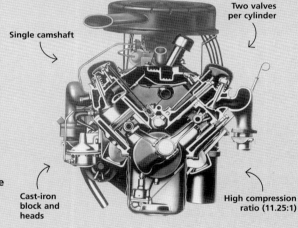

Single camshaft

Two valves per cylinder

Cast-iron block and heads

High compression ratio (11.25:1)

Long and low

The 1959 Impala was designed to look as long and low as possible. Today, this makes it a popular choice for those who want to build a lowrider. By bringing the car closer to the ground, the Impala's low lines are accentuated even further.

The sleek and elegant Impala was a big car even by 1959 standards.

Chevrolet IMPALA

Top of the 1959 Chevrolet range, the Impala had it all—wild styling, luxury fittings, and a huge amount of horsepower. It makes an ideal choice for a stylish custom lowrider.

Big-block engine

Introduced in 1958, the 348-cubic inch V8 is capable of producing astounding power outputs. The top 1959 engine produces 315 bhp.

Huge trunk

The 1959 Impala has one of the biggest trunks ever made by Chevrolet. The wheelbase was increased 3.9 inch between 1956 and 1959.

Ground-hugging stance

This Impala's low-slung appearance has been achieved without modifying the suspension. The owner has simply fitted 13-inch wheels instead of the stock 14-inch rims. The factory spring length remains unaltered.

Factory custom

Although this car looks highly customized, all the modifications (except for the wheels) were factory options. A buyer could have ordered an Impala like this in 1959, but few customers specified this many options. It has side skirts, spot lights, a continental kit, bumper guards, remote trunk release, cruise control, air-conditioning, and power-assisted everything.

Coil-sprung rear axle

The Impala has a simple rear suspension set-up. The live rear axle is coil-sprung with telescopic shocks. In order to prevent wheel hop, Chevrolet engineers added trailing arms, a Panhard rod, and a central torque reaction arm to locate the rear axle.

Wild style

The 1959 Impala must rate as the wildest-looking Chevrolet ever even rivaling the overtly-stylized 1959 Cadillac. Chevrolet tamed the car's appearance for 1960 with revised front and rear styling.

Continental kit

The continental kit was a highly desirable option on late-1950s cars. Although it was fitted mainly for aesthetic appeal, it does have a practical use. By mounting the spare wheel behind the rear bumper, more trunk space is available for luggage.

Specifications
1959 Chevrolet Impala

ENGINE

Type: V8

Construction: Cast-iron block and heads

Valve gear: Two valves per cylinder operated by a single central camshaft

Bore and stroke: 4.133 in. x 3.26 in.

Displacement: 348 c.i.

Compression ratio: 11.25:1

Induction system: Three two-barrel Rochester carburetors

Maximum power: 315 bhp at 5,600 rpm

Maximum torque: 357 lb-ft at 3,600 rpm

Top speed: 134 mph

0-60 mph: 9.0 sec.

TRANSMISSION

Optional three- or four-speed manual or two-speed automatic

BODY/CHASSIS

Steel box-section cruciform chassis with two-door convertible body

SPECIAL FEATURES

These wide, low-profile chrome wire wheels are particularly eye-catching.

The continental kit looks smart, but it adds more than 11 inches to the car's overall length.

RUNNING GEAR

Steering: Recirculating ball

Front suspension: Double wishbones with coil springs and telescopic shocks

Rear suspension: Live axle with coil springs and telescopic shocks

Brakes: Four-wheel drums

Wheels: Wire wheels, 13-in. dia.

Tires: 155/80 R14

DIMENSIONS

Length: 223.4 in.   **Width:** 80 in.

Height: 57 in.   **Wheelbase:** 119 in.

Track: 60.2 in. (front), 59.5 in. (rear)

Weight: 3,649 lbs.

Chevrolet **INDEPENDENCE**

It is well known that early-1930s cars make great hot rods. But going several steps beyond the traditional format is this unique, awesome five-window coupe which, with its thunderous V8 engine and lightning acceleration, justifiably lives up to its name, 'Wild Thang.'

"...feel the ground shake."

"Looking like a refugee from a comic strip, this Chevy is like no other. The mighty motor explodes into life with a thunderous roar, and through open headers you can almost feel the ground shake. On the road, this car is a sight tobehold. It turns heads everywhere it goes, but one thing will be etched in your memory—the acceleration. This rod will rocket to 60 mph in just under 5 seconds and is guaranteed to bring a smile."

Twin JAZ racing buckets and harnesses keep the occupants firmly in place.

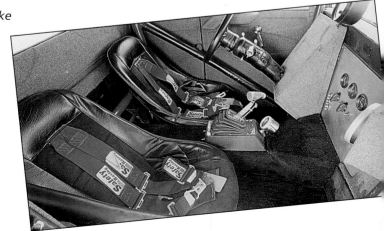

Milestones

1931 Despite a model name change

to Independence, the Chevrolet range is little changed from 1929, with almost Cadillac-like styling. Prices, however, are anything but, ranging from $475 to $650.

Chevrolets were popular in 1931 —this is a Police Sedan Delivery.

1932 In keeping with the

yearly model change, the Confederate displaces the Independence. As before, all Chevrolets rely on the 127-cubic inches for power. Despite the onset of the Depression, 306,716 Chevrolets leave the assembly line.

The big 454 V8 gained prominence in the SS Chevelle.

1933 Chevrolet diversifies

and introduces two new series—the Eagle on a 110-inch wheelbase chassis, and the Mercury with a 107.5-inch wheelbase.

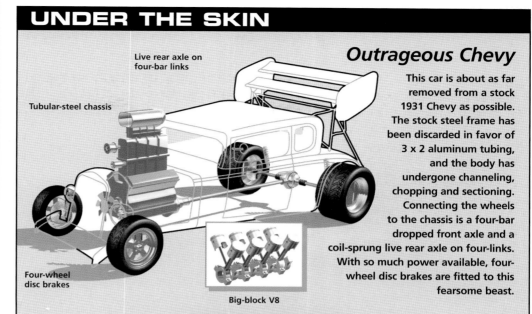

Live rear axle on four-bar links

Tubular-steel chassis

Four-wheel disc brakes

Big-block V8

Outrageous Chevy

This car is about as far removed from a stock 1931 Chevy as possible. The stock steel frame has been discarded in favor of 3 x 2 aluminum tubing, and the body has undergone channeling, chopping and sectioning. Connecting the wheels to the chassis is a four-bar dropped front axle and a coil-sprung live rear axle on four-links. With so much power available, four-wheel disc brakes are fitted to this fearsome beast.

THE POWER PACK

Overkill

In place of the 194-cubic inch six, with its 50 bhp, is a motor with a very different character. Above the firewall and radiator shell is a 454-cubic inch big-block overbored by 0.030 inch. Atop the block sit a Weiand intake manifold and a custom-built intercooler, mated to a 6-71 Weiand positive displacement supercharger. To enable this setup to run with reliability, the block carries eight 8.5:1-compression pistons, and fuel is fed through two massive Holley 750-cfm Double Pumper four-barrel carburetors. Spent gases are exhausted through eight individual pipes, directly from the engine exhaust ports.

Coupe to go

Not as popular with the street contingent as contemporary Fords, the early-1930s Chevrolets still have great potential for hot-rodding, and just about anything can be done with them. This radical 1931 five-window coupe is faster than many exotic supercars and will turn more heads on the sidewalk. Best of all, it is a unique and personal vehicle.

The term "extreme" is truly appropriate for this Chevy.

Chevrolet INDEObviously **INDEPENDENCE**

It is very difficult to know what to make of this car. Its appearance suggests that it was built strictly for show, but it is a fully functioning 200-mph-plus street rod that is also street-legal.

Killer V8 engine

The big 460-cubic inch V8, with its twin carburetors and massive intercooler/supercharger setup is enough to strike fear into the heart of any fellow hot-rodder.

Chopped top

The top has been chopped, which reduces its height. This also has the effect of exaggerating the height of the engine.

Aluminum rear wing

Because this car is capable of such incredible acceleration and speed, it needs to be kept firmly planted to the road in order to prevent rear-end liftoff. A huge aluminum rear wing, similar to those found on Outlaw sprint cars, ensures the rear end stays on the ground at high speeds.

Straight pipes

Projecting from each cylinder head are individual exhaust pipes. They help the engine make an owner-estimated 900 bhp and contribute to the big V8's earth-shattering sound.

Widened body

A modification on this rod is the widening of the rear bodywork. It now measures an extra 3 inches across.

Parachute

Packed up behind the wheelie bars is a parachute that helps slow the car down after it reaches its maximum speed.

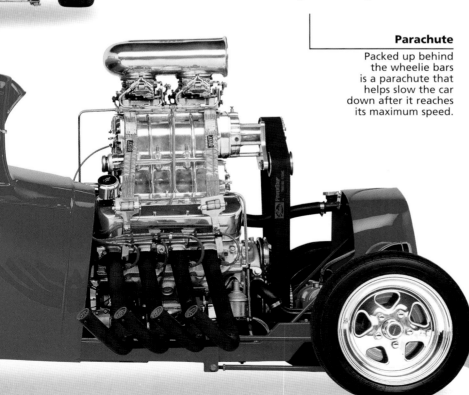

Specifications

1931 Chevrolet Independence

ENGINE

Type: V8

Construction: Cast-iron block and heads

Valve gear: Two valves per cylinder operated by a single V-mounted camshaft with pushrods and rockers

Bore and stroke: 4.28 in. x 4.00 in.

Displacement: 460 c.i.

Compression ratio: 8.5:1

Induction system: Dual Holley 750 DM four-barrel carburetors

Maximum power: 900 bhp at 6,400 rpm

Maximum torque: 710 lb-ft at 3,800 rpm

Top speed: 170 mph

0-60 mph: 4.5 sec.

TRANSMISSION

TH400 three-speed automatic

BODY/CHASSIS

Steel tubular chassis with two-door coupe body

SPECIAL FEATURES

The whole engine assembly has been chrome-plated for maximum impact.

Wheelie bars help protect the rear pan when the throttle is mashed.

RUNNING GEAR

Steering: Recirculating-ball

Front suspension: Beam axle with transverse leaf spring, four-bar links and telescopic shock absorbers

Rear suspension: Live axle with four-bar links, coil springs and coil-over shock absorbers

Brakes: Discs (front and rear)

Wheels: Cragar Drag Star, 15 x 7 in. (front), 15 x 15 in. (rear)

Tires: BFGoodrich, 195/50 15 (front), Mickey Thompson, 29/18.5 15 (rear)

DIMENSIONS

Length: 152.6 in.   **Width:** 74.7 in.

Height: 58.5 in.   **Wheelbase:** 109.0 in.

Track: 51.3 in. (front), 57.1 in. (rear)

Weight: 2,850 lbs.

Chevrolet MONTE CARLO

A big seller in the 1970s, the third-generation Monte Carlo has become especially popular in recent years with the lowrider community. Some of these cars are turned into works of automotive art.

"...reserved for special occasions."

"You can tell just by looking that this car is reserved for special occasions. There is no dash—instead the firewall panel is covered in buttoned velour upholstery. Then there's the absence of side glass and B-pillars. Performance is average, but this car is all about looks. Watch passersby crane their necks as you glide along the street. Flick the switches and feel the car dance. Lowrider is an automotive culture unlike any other."

The whole interior is color coordinated in four-tone velour upholstery.

Milestones

1973 A second-generation
Monte Carlo on a new G-body platform arrives. With its curvy sheet metal it is a big hit and finds 290,693 buyers.

The Monte Carlo has the longest hood ever fitted to a Chevy®.

1976 Having proved a success,
the Monte Carlo is mildly facelifted with stacked headlights and a new grill, plus slight alterations to the interior. The big-block 454 engine option is dropped.

1978 Following in the footsteps
of the full-size cars, GM intermediates are downsized, including the Malibu™ and related Monte Carlo.

A second-generation Monte Carlo arrived for 1973.

1980 The Monte Carlo is
facelifted at the front with quad headlights. A crisp restyle marks the 1981 Monte Carlo.

UNDER THE SKIN

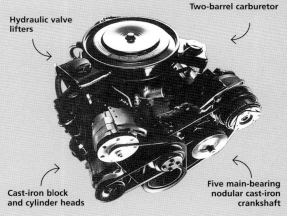

Body-on-the-frame construction

Double wishbone front suspension

Hydraulic rams front and rear

Small-block V8

Corporate coupe

Built off the GM G-body platform which also included the Oldsmobile® Cutlass™ and Pontiac® Grand Prix™ coupes, the Monte Carlo has a separate chassis and steel body. There is a wishbone front suspension, while at the rear is a oil-sprung live axle, both coil sprung. Modifications included fitting hydraulic rams on the front and rear control arms and lowering the ride height by 4 inches at the front and 3.5 inches at the rear.

THE POWER PACK

Smog-restricted V8

Back in 1979, America was in the depths of a fuel crisis so the Monte Carlo left the factory with either a 200-cubic inch Chevy, a 231-cubic inch Buick V6 or 305-cubic inch small-block V8. The latter is a destroked 350 and was rushed out in 1975 in response to the first energy crisis. With exhaust gas recirculation, restrictive exhaust manifolds and a two-barrel carburetor, it puts out just 120 bhp. However, with 240 lb-ft of torque it makes the Monte a fine long-distance cruiser. This engine remains stock.

Hydraulic valve lifters

Two-barrel carburetor

Cast-iron block and cylinder heads

Five main-bearing nodular cast-iron crankshaft

Plentiful

These cars were tremendously popular when new, and simple, rugged engineering with a plentiful and inexpensive parts supply means that they make a practical buy today. These cars make excellent starting points for one-of-a-kind customs.

1978-1980 Monte Carlos are a favorite choice for lowrider enthusiasts.

Chevrolet **MONTE CARLO**

East Los Angeles is the center for the lowrider movement and boasts some of the finest cars anywhere. This 1979 Monte Carlo is no exception and can be regarded as a benchmark for lowrider aficionados.

Body modifications

The unmistakable baroque styling of the late-1970s Monte Carlo is still there, but has been considerably altered. The side glass and B-pillars have been completely removed, turning this Monte into a true hardtop.

V8 engine

Back in the late 1970s, V6s and economically tuned small-block V8s were the norm in most American cars. This Monte Carlo is no exception, being fitted with a 305-cubic inch (5.0-liter) V8 with a two-barrel carburetor.

Updated front end

Appearances can be deceptive, for although this Monte Carlo has a 1980 nose piece, it is a 1979 model. The owner choose to fit this nose in order to stand out from the crowd. The major changes for 1980 were quad headlights and repositioned turn signal/running lights.

Modified suspension

All true lowriders have customized suspensions that are able to raise and lower the car by using an 8-inch hydraulic pump. This system replaces the stock suspension and is activated by three car batteries.

Wild paint

Perhaps the greatest attention was applied to the paint finish. A rough texture base coat was applied, followed by 'School Bus' yellow pearl and accentuated by five shades of yellow/orange pearl and gold pinstriping. The result is striking, to say the least.

Separate chassis

Although it may seem antiquated, having a separate chassis saved on tooling costs and enabled a soft ride and reduced vibration on the road—an important selling point for what was, after all, a personal luxury coupe.

Lounge-style interior

The interior has also been totally reworked, including the removal of the dashboard and all the gauges. A custom center console with a built-in TV has been fabricated and the interior cockpit trimmed with crushed velour.

Specifications

1979 Chevrolet Monte Carlo

ENGINE
Type: V8
Construction: Cast-iron block and heads
Valve gear: Two valves per cylinder operated by pushrods and rockers
Bore and stroke: 3.74 in. x 3.48 in.
Displacement: 305 c.i.
Compression ratio: 8.6:1
Induction system: Rochester two-barrel carburetor
Maximum power: 120 bhp at 3,800 rpm
Maximum torque: 240 lb-ft at 2,400 rpm
Top speed: 118 mph
0-60 mph: 9.4 sec

TRANSMISSION
GM 2004-R three-speed automatic

BODY/CHASSIS
Separate steel chassis with two-door body

SPECIAL FEATURES

Dayton chrome 13-inch wire wheels are a must for any lowrider.

Swivel front seats hark back to the larger 1973-1977 Monte Carlos.

RUNNING GEAR
Steering: Recirculating ball
Front suspension: Unequal length wishbones with coil springs, telescopic shock absorbers and anti-roll bar
Rear suspension: Live axle with coil springs and telescopic shock absorbers
Brakes: Discs (front), drums (rear)
Wheels: Dayton wires, 7 x 13 in. (front and rear)
Tires: Premium Sportway, 5 x 13 in.

DIMENSIONS
Length: 189.5 in.   **Width:** 79.8 in.
Height: 51.4 in.   **Wheelbase:** 108.1 in.
Track: 64.6 in. (front), 65.7 in. (rear)
Weight: 3,169 lbs.

Chevrolet **NOMAD**

One of the most stylish wagons of all time, the 1955-1957 Chevrolet Nomads are a favorite with both collectors and customizers. The owner of this car has taken a traditional approach when customizing his 1956 Nomad.

"...supercharged performance."

"With its bucket seats and thick-rimmed steering wheel, this 1956 Nomad has a sporty edge. Push down on the throttle and feel its supercharged performance that can only come from a 1970 Corvette® small-block V8 with a B&M blower. It rockets the car to 60 mph in less than six seconds. No expense has been spared underneath either, and the 1986 Corvette suspension enables this car to corner much better than it did stock.

The dashboard is original, but the Connolly leather bucket seats have been added and give the car a more upmarket feel.

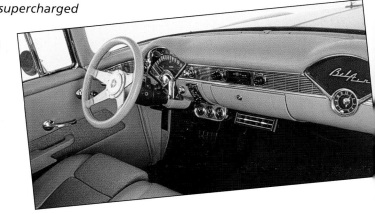

Milestones

1955 Chevrolet
announces its new models, totally restyled and with magnificent new V8 engines. Top of the range is the distinctive Nomad, combining hardtop styling with station wagon practicality.

Designed by Carl Renner, the Nomad first appeared in 1955.

1956 Performance
is improved with up to 265 bhp available from the small-block V8. Nomads, like the rest of the line, adopt busier styling.

The Nomad was subtly restyled for the 1956 model year.

1957 The two-door
Nomad is again listed and receives another, and arguably more attractive, facelift. A Ramjet mechanical fuel injection system is available with the 283 V8 giving up to 283 bhp. Due to its high cost, its two-door styling and several seal problems, sales are moderate. Chevrolet decides to drop the model for its 1958 model line-up.

UNDER THE SKIN

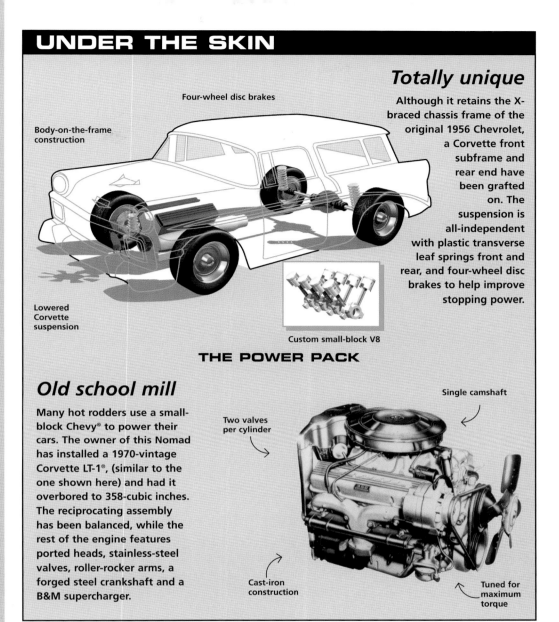

Four-wheel disc brakes

Body-on-the-frame construction

Lowered Corvette suspension

Custom small-block V8

THE POWER PACK

Totally unique

Although it retains the X-braced chassis frame of the original 1956 Chevrolet, a Corvette front subframe and rear end have been grafted on. The suspension is all-independent with plastic transverse leaf springs front and rear, and four-wheel disc brakes to help improve stopping power.

Old school mill

Many hot rodders use a small-block Chevy® to power their cars. The owner of this Nomad has installed a 1970-vintage Corvette LT-1®, (similar to the one shown here) and had it overbored to 358-cubic inches. The reciprocating assembly has been balanced, while the rest of the engine features ported heads, stainless-steel valves, roller-rocker arms, a forged steel crankshaft and a B&M supercharger.

Two valves per cylinder

Single camshaft

Cast-iron construction

Tuned for maximum torque

The Cormad

Although it looks like a mild custom, this Nomad has been drastically modified. Underneath is a 1986 Corvette front and rear suspension, complete with brakes and shocks. With a reworked LT-1 engine, this car will surprise many drivers on the road.

With their classic lines, Shoebox-Chevy Nomads are collector's favorites.

Chevrolet NOMAD

This Shoebox-Chevy Nomad combines style with performance. Using a Corvette powerplant and running gear, this 1956 Nomad can surprise many newer performance cars.

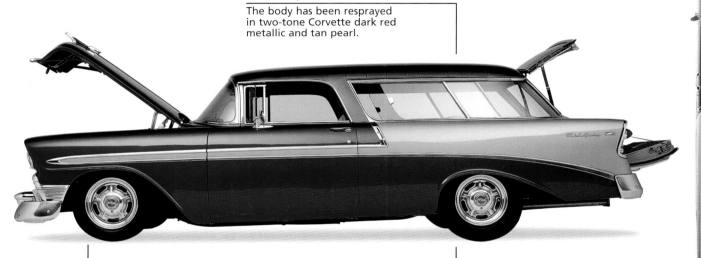

Modern paint

The body has been resprayed in two-tone Corvette dark red metallic and tan pearl.

Modified transmission

A 1976 Turbo 400 automatic transmission backs up the sinister LT1 engine. To extract maximum power from the engine, it has a high-stall torque converter.

Custom wheels

No street machine would be complete without aftermarket wheels. This Nomad is fitted with a set of custom chromed 16-inch wheels.

Clean lines

Even in 1956, the Nomad was a fairly clean-looking car. The two-tone paintwork and chrome spears accentuate the classic lines of this Chevrolet.

Corvette front end

The front suspension employs a 1986 Corvette subframe. Not only does it lower the car, giving it a ground-hugging stance, but it greatly improves the car's handling.

Small-block power

For massive performance, this ubiquitous 1970 LT-1 small-block V8 has been bored over .060-inch in and features a forged-steel crank, ported and polished cylinder heads, roller rocker arms plus a B&M supercharger and a Holley carburetor.

Specifications

1956 Chevrolet Nomad

ENGINE

Type: V8

Construction: Cast-iron block and heads

Valve gear: Two valves per cylinder operated by pushrods and rockers

Bore and stroke: 4.06 in. x 3.48 in.

Displacement: 358 c.i.

Compression ratio: 10.5:1

Induction system: B&M supercharger and Holley four-barrel carburetor

Maximum power: 400 bhp at 4,800 rpm

Maximum torque: 320 lb-ft at 3,000 rpm

Top speed: 131 mph

0-60 mph: 5.5 sec.

TRANSMISSION

1976 Turbo HydraMatic 400 with a high-stall torque converter

BODY/CHASSIS

Separate two-door station wagon steel body on X-braced steel frame and Corvette front subframe.

SPECIAL FEATURES

The fuel cap is neatly hidden behind the tail light.

With the rear seat folded down, luggage space is cavernous.

RUNNING GEAR

Steering: Recirculating ball

Front suspension: Double wishbones with plastic transverse leaf spring and shocks

Rear suspension: Trailing arms with plastic transverse leaf spring and shocks

Brakes: Discs (front and rear)

Wheels: Custom Boyds, 15-in. dia.

Tires: Goodyear P22560VR15

DIMENSIONS

Length: 196.7 in. **Width:** 77.2 in.

Height: 53 in. **Wheelbase:** 115 in.

Track: 59.5 in. (front), 55.8 in. (rear)

Weight: 3,352 lbs.

DeSoto FIREFLITE

The name may have long passed into the annals of history, but that still does not stop a small but ardent band of followers from restoring and maintaining these great cars. The Fireflite is a one-of-a-kind street machine.

"...exceedingly quick."

"Every now and then it's nice to try something different, and this Fireflite is it. The capacious interior has been tastefully altered, and although it is stock, the Hemi V8 is powerful and the Fireflite is exceedingly quick in a straight line. The automatic transmission is excellent for a car of this era, effortlessly shifting between gears. By modern standards, the steering is very light and the ride soft, but when cruising, these factors pale into insignificance."

There's no shortage of flair in the way the cabin has been finished on this 'special.'

Milestones

1949 The all-new
DeSotos arrive in March. The power of the straight-six engine is 112 bhp. A total of 94,371 new models are built.

1952 DeSoto's first-
ever V8, of 276 cubic inches with 160 bhp, arrives. V8 models are more popular than the six-cylinder Custom/Deluxe variants.

By 1939, DeSoto offered only closed bodystyles.

1955 New, more
aggressive styling spruces up the line.

1956 The standard
Hemi is bored out to 330 cubic inches with 230 bhp in Firedomes and 255 bhp in Fireflites. The 'Adventurer' hardtop is given a 320-bhp engine.

The 1955 DeSoto Adventurer II was an exotic Ghia-styled four-seater show car.

1957 An all-new
range of heavily redesigned DeSotos is launched.

UNDER THE SKIN

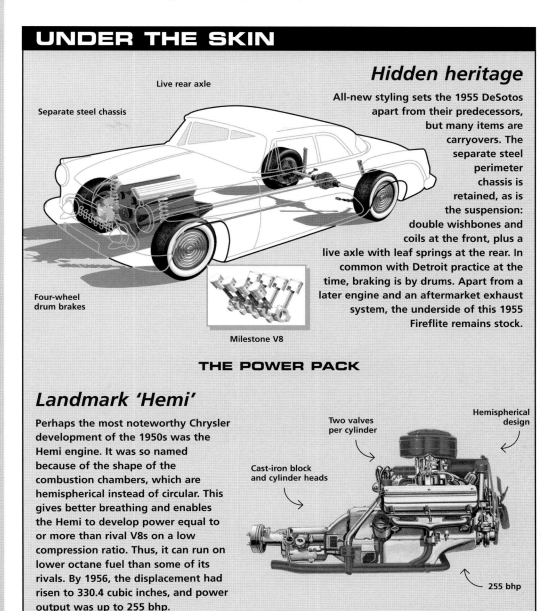

Live rear axle

Separate steel chassis

Four-wheel drum brakes

Milestone V8

Hidden heritage

All-new styling sets the 1955 DeSotos apart from their predecessors, but many items are carryovers. The separate steel perimeter chassis is retained, as is the suspension: double wishbones and coils at the front, plus a live axle with leaf springs at the rear. In common with Detroit practice at the time, braking is by drums. Apart from a later engine and an aftermarket exhaust system, the underside of this 1955 Fireflite remains stock.

THE POWER PACK

Landmark 'Hemi'

Perhaps the most noteworthy Chrysler development of the 1950s was the Hemi engine. It was so named because of the shape of the combustion chambers, which are hemispherical instead of circular. This gives better breathing and enables the Hemi to develop power equal to or more than rival V8s on a low compression ratio. Thus, it can run on lower octane fuel than some of its rivals. By 1956, the displacement had risen to 330.4 cubic inches, and power output was up to 255 bhp.

Two valves per cylinder

Hemispherical design

Cast-iron block and cylinder heads

255 bhp

Adventurer

If there is a favorite among the 1955-1956 DeSotos, it is the high-performance Adventurer, but with only 996 built, it is rare. Besides this, the Fireflite Sportsman hardtop is an ideal choice, with its handsome lines and 200-/255-bhp V8.

Fireflite Sportsmans have sharp styling and offer plenty of V8 power.

DeSoto FIREFLITE

Even in their day, these cars were considered flamboyant, to say the least, but this period-modified example takes the idea a step further with its stunning paint finish and classic custom touches.

Custom paint

This Fireflite has been painted using DuPont Sonic Purple as the main color, with the roof and lower rear fenders covered in contrasting Eggshell White. This two-tone combination is well suited to the sweeping lines.

Hemi V8

Although this car originally came with a Hemi V8, the original engine is long gone. In its place is a 1956 330 Hemi. Unlike many other street machines, which have radically modified engines, the owner chose to leave the V8 stock. With 255 bhp, however, performance is still far from sedate.

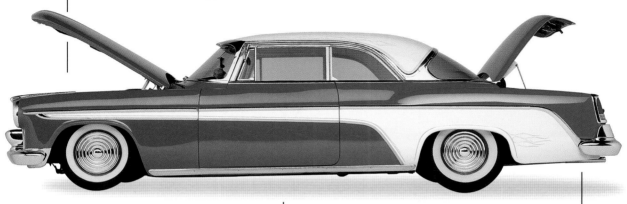

Swoopy styling

DeSotos were fairly stodgy-looking cars until 1955. Although all Chryslers were restyled that year, the DeSotos benefited most of all. Some even claimed these cars were among the most beautiful automobiles ever to come out of Detroit.

Aftermarket exhaust

In the 1950s and 1960s, it was common for many speed freaks to fit aftermarket exhausts to help the engine produce more power. This DeSoto has a classic stainless-steel system with true dual pipes and glass pack mufflers. This results in an extra 7 bhp and makes for a terrific-sounding engine.

Shaved and smoothed body

A popular modification on many cars of the 1940s and 1950s is to smooth the body, accentuating the sheet metal contours. On this Fireflite, the body has been nosed and decked, and all emblems and the door handles have been removed.

Specifications

1955 DeSoto Fireflite Sportsman

ENGINE

Type: V8

Construction: Cast-iron block and heads

Valve gear: Two valves per cylinder operated by a singe camshaft via pushrods and rockers

Bore and stroke: 3.72 in. x 3.80 in.

Displacement: 330.4 c.i.

Compression ratio: 10.0:1

Induction system: Dual four-barrel carburetors

Maximum power: 255 bhp at 5,200 rpm

Maximum torque: 340 lb-ft at 2,800 rpm

Top speed: 118 mph

0-60 mph: 8.2 sec.

TRANSMISSION

TorqueFlite three-speed automatic

BODY/CHASSIS

Separate steel chassis with two-door hardtop body

SPECIAL FEATURES

Half-moon headlight covers are a typical custom feature for this kind of car.

In DeSotos, the Hemi V8 was known as the Firedome Eight.

RUNNING GEAR

Steering: Recirculating ball

Front suspension: Unequal-length wishbones with coil springs and telescopic shock absorbers

Rear suspension: Live axle with semi-elliptic multi-leaf springs and telescopic shock absorbers

Brakes: Drums (front and rear)

Wheels: Steel discs, 5 x 14 in.

Tires: F70-14

DIMENSIONS

Length: 204.0 in. **Width:** 85.4 in.

Height: 58.9 in. **Wheelbase:** 126.0 in

Track: 65.7 in. (front), 63.2 in. (rear)

Weight: 3,930 lbs.

Toothy grill

The distinctive grill treatment is a trademark of DeSotos from 1953 to 1955. This car's owner has retained it but has modified the front bumper.

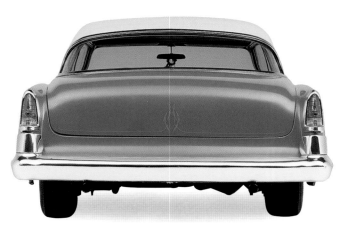

Two-tone interior

Many 1950s cars had factory interiors that matched the two-tone exterior. Although the paint finish on this car is not stock, the owner has chosen a matching interior. The seats and doors are Eggshell White, with purple inserts in the headlining.

Dodge **CHARGER**

Based on the intermediate Coronet, the Charger created a sensation when it arrived for 1966. The dramatic fastback shape also lends it to custom modifications, as demonstrated by this example.

"...modernized muscle car."

"This modified Charger is a uniquely modernized classic muscle car. The interior still looks cool, even today, and with a small-block, 360-cubic inch V8, performance is better than average. 0-60 mph takes just eight seconds and, thanks to its relatively tall gearing, this Charger can cruise happily at 100 mph. With a lowered suspension and modern tires, it holds the road too, and front disc brakes mean it stops far better than with the original drums."

A Le Carrera steering wheel and Auto Meter gauges give it a roadracing flair.

Milestones

1966 The Charger is launched
as a stylish two-door fastback based on the intermediate Coronet 117-inch wheelbase chassis. Flashy touches include a hidden headlight grill and a four-bucket-seat interior. Engines range from a 318-cubic inch unit to the monster 425-bhp, 426 Hemi.

A second-generation Charger arrived for 1968. This is the limited production 1969 500.

1967 After selling
37,344 units in its debut year, the Charger returns with few changes. A new performance-oriented R/T package arrives with a standard 440-cubic inch V8 and heavy-duty suspension. Sales drop to 15,788 in its sophomore year.

A Ram pickup donated its 360 V8 for this particular Charger.

1968 An all-new, Coke-bottle
styled, second-generation Charger arrives.

UNDER THE SKIN

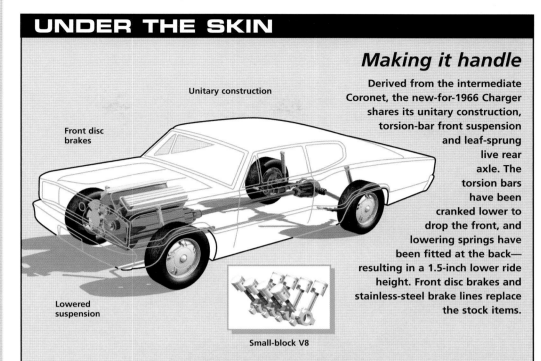

Unitary construction

Front disc brakes

Lowered suspension

Small-block V8

Making it handle

Derived from the intermediate Coronet, the new-for-1966 Charger shares its unitary construction, torsion-bar front suspension and leaf-sprung live rear axle. The torsion bars have been cranked lower to drop the front, and lowering springs have been fitted at the back—resulting in a 1.5-inch lower ride height. Front disc brakes and stainless-steel brake lines replace the stock items.

THE POWER PACK

Mid-1970s muscle

Back in 1966, this Charger had a 318-cubic inch V8 nestling between the fenders. Now long gone, the original V8 has been replaced with something a little more potent: a 1978 360-cubic inch engine taken from a Dodge Ram pickup. This 360, which is an excellent high-performance V8 in its own right, has been further improved with the aid of Sealed Power pistons, a high-lift Mopar Performance camshaft, Edelbrock performer intake manifold and four-barrel carburetor. Retaining the stock manifolds, the V8 delivers 365 bhp at 4,700 rpm and 400 lb-ft of torque, making an excellent, head-turning driver.

Base model

Most common of the first-generation Chargers are the 1966 models. The big-block cars are the most sought after, but regular examples are cheaper to buy and are more readily available. They easily accept more power and can be modified to handle well, too.

Eclipsed in popularity by later Chargers, the early cars are still a good buy.

Dodge CHARGER

First generation Chargers almost beg for custom treatment, and even with subtle modifications they are guaranteed head-turners on the street. This one has won numerous awards at shows and cruises.

More modern engine

For reasons of practicality, the owner has fitted a small-block, 360-cubic inch V8 of late-1970s vintage. It has been mildly reworked with an aftermarket intake and carb, a hotter camshaft and late-model ignition.

Fastback roof

Although essentially a Coronet with a fastback roof, the 1966 Charger evidently proved to be a hit, with 37,344 sold that year.

Lowered suspension

Although this car retains the stock suspension, it has been lowered. The front torsion bars have been cranked down and lowering blocks fitted on the rear leaf springs, reducing its ride height. This means cornering limits are far greater than Chrysler could have imagined in the 1960s.

Unitary construction

Like all intermediate Mopars built in the mid- and late-1960s, the Charger has a unitary body/chassis resulting in a stiffer structure than that of some of its rivals.

Updated interior

Besides late-model seats, the transmission shift indicator on the console has been modified to read Skully (the car's name), instead of the normal P-R-N-D-2-1 pattern.

Low-profile tires

Besides the lowered suspension, modern BF Goodrich radial tires improve handling even further. Those at the rear are slightly larger than those at the front (255/45x17 versus 215/45x17), which gives excellent traction during standing-start acceleration.

Specifications

1966 Dodge Charger

ENGINE
Type: V8

Construction: Cast-iron block and heads

Valve gear: Two valves per cylinder operated by a single camshaft with pushrods and rocker arms

Bore and stroke: 4.00 in. x 3.58 in.

Displacement: 360 c.i.

Compression ratio: 9.1:1

Induction system: Edelbrock Performer four-barrel downdraft carburetor

Maximum power: 365 bhp at 4,700 rpm

Maximum torque: 400 lb-ft at 2,800 rpm

Top speed: 135 mph

0-60 mph: 8.0 sec

TRANSMISSION
TorqueFlite three-speed automatic

BODY/CHASSIS
Unitary steel chassis with two-door fastback body

SPECIAL FEATURES

Given the nickname 'Skully,' this car has subtle custom body graphics.

Full-length dual exhaust pipes help the 360 V8 produce its 365 bhp.

RUNNING GEAR
Steering: Recirculating ball

Front suspension: Unequal-length A-arms with torsion bars, telescopic shock absorbers and anti-roll bar

Rear suspension: Live axle with semi-elliptic leaf springs and telescopic shock absorbers

Brakes: Discs (front), drums (rear)

Wheels: Centerline Scorpion, 7 x 17 in. (front), 8 x 17 in. (rear)

Tires: BF Goodrich Comp ZR, 215/45x17 (front), 255/45x17 (rear)

DIMENSIONS
Length: 204.2 in.   **Width:** 75.0 in.

Height: 55.2 in.   **Wheelbase:** 117.0 in.

Track: 59.5 in. (front), 58.5 in. (rear)

Weight: 3,900 lbs.

Ford ANGLIA GASSER

As drag racing began to blossom during the early 1950s, hot-rodders were looking for suitable cars to modify for ¼-mile duty. The old ultra-light Fords proved ideal and were frequent winners on the drag strip.

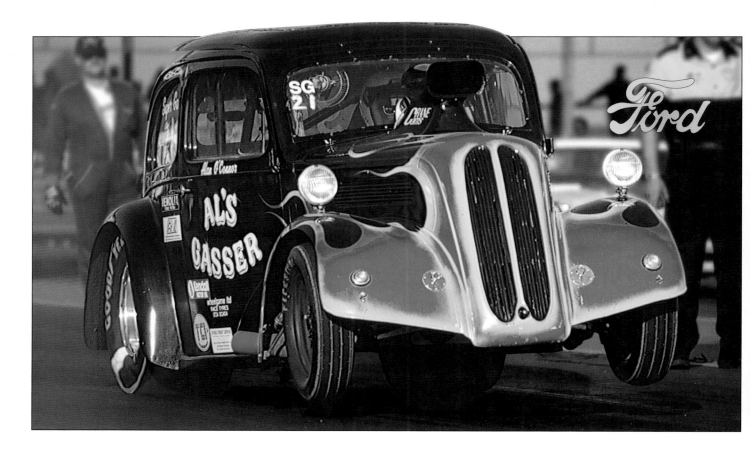

"...shoots forward."

"It is more like stepping into an aircraft than a car. The steering and seats are positioned well back and there is aluminum paneling everywhere. The acceleration is unbelievable and so is the noise. Immediately after the accelerator drops to the floor, nitrous oxide is sprayed into the engine's combustion chambers for one hundred extra bhp. The front end lifts off the ground as the rear slicks dig into the pavement."

This is where it all happens. The gauges alert the driver as to what the engine is doing as the car nears 170 mph.

Milestones

1937 The model 7Y is unique
in being the first English-built Ford that is also designed in Britain. It boasts a new chassis with a longer spring base for an improved ride and handling.

The Anglia was replaced by a more modern monocoque model.

1939 Basically a squared-up
version of the 7Y, the Anglia is the first in a long line of cars with this famous name. Only 5,136 are built before war halts production in early 1941. Production resumes in 1944, although most of these cars are exported.

The Willys Coupe is also a popular basis for a 'gasser' car.

1948 A new Anglia, which is
almost identical to the old 7Y except for a protruding trunk and different grill, appears. U.S. version models have larger engines. A total of 387,351 have been built by the time production ends in 1953.

UNDER THE SKIN

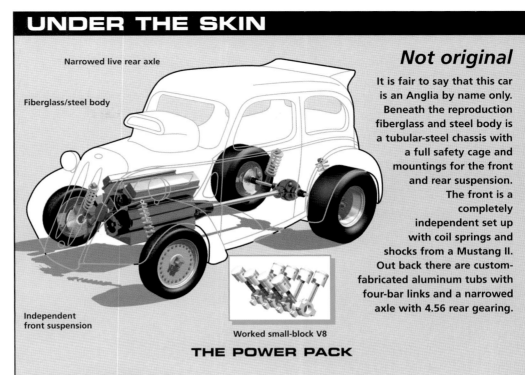

Narrowed live rear axle

Fiberglass/steel body

Independent front suspension

Worked small-block V8

Not original

It is fair to say that this car is an Anglia by name only. Beneath the reproduction fiberglass and steel body is a tubular-steel chassis with a full safety cage and mountings for the front and rear suspension. The front is a completely independent set up with coil springs and shocks from a Mustang II. Out back there are custom-fabricated aluminum tubs with four-bar links and a narrowed axle with 4.56 rear gearing.

THE POWER PACK

Custom-built V8

In place of the tiny, wheezy four-cylinder, this car is fitted with a Chevrolet small-block (stock unit shown here). This 1972 350-cubic inch unit has been almost completely reworked, with custom free-flowing cylinder heads, stainless-steel valves, a single plane Edelbrock high-riser intake manifold, a huge 850-cfm Holley carburetor, a forged-steel custom ground crankshaft, heavy-duty connecting rods and a Lunati camshaft. When combined with the wet nitrous system, this results in a total output of 775 bhp.

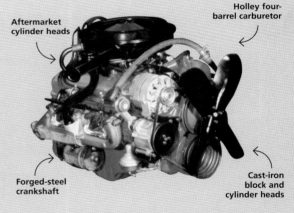

Aftermarket cylinder heads

Holley four-barrel carburetor

Forged-steel crankshaft

Cast-iron block and cylinder heads

Light and fast

Anglias are popular with many racers. They are small and light, plus plenty of specialist race car outfits can supply replica bodies and build custom chassis and engines to order. Properly prepared Anglias are some of the quickest cars at the drags.

Anglias are an excellent choice for stock-bodied drag cars.

Ford ANGLIA GASSER

This example is typical of the Anglias currently competing in regional and national sanctioned drag events. Some of these cars can run low 8-second elapsed times over the ¼-mile.

Custom-fabricated interior

The driver is surrounded by a roll cage which makes for an incredibly stiff structure. A set of Auto Meter gauges and a monster tach keep the driver informed. A five-point harness and fire extinguisher are mandatory for sanctioned drag racing.

Custom rear suspension

Like many drag cars, the rear end is heavily modified with a narrowed 9-inch Ford rear axle and upper and lower links with twin coil springs and telescopic shocks. The whole system pivots up and down to enable the tires to have maximum contact with the pavement at all times.

Chevrolet V8

Many hot-rodders and racers use Chevrolet small-block V8s to power their Anglias. These engines have become so popular that a variety of parts are available from aftermarket high-performance companies that make parts strictly for racing.

Braking parachute

Because of the incredible speeds reached in Pro-Gas class racing, a parachute is essential for stopping the Anglia once it has crossed the line. In NHRA sanctioned ¼ mile racing a parachute is required if a car reaches 150 mph or faster.

Fiberglass body

The body is a fiberglass/steel reproduction which closely follows the outline of the original car. Fiberglass is popular because it is light, easy to mold and fairly simple to replace.

Sponsor graphics

Racing is an expensive business and most drag racers require sponsorship. This purple Anglia Gasser is painted in the colors of a security company that sponsors the racing team. The orange tag hanging from the parachute box is a required safety device that keeps the chute from opening up when the car is not racing. It is removed right before the car races.

Specifications

1951 Ford Anglia Gasser

ENGINE
Type: V8
Construction: Cast-iron block and heads
Valve gear: Two valves per cylinder operated by pushrods and rockers
Bore and stroke: 4.00 in. x 3.48 in.
Displacement: 350 c.i.
Compression ratio: 12.5:1
Induction system: Holley four-barrel carburetor, nitrous oxide system
Maximum power: 775 bhp at 6,200 rpm
Maximum torque: 680 lb-ft at 4,000 rpm
Top speed: 170 mph
0-60 mph: 2.4 sec

TRANSMISSION
Jericho four-speed manual

BODY/CHASSIS
Tubular-steel chassis with fiberglass/steel two-door sedan body

SPECIAL FEATURES

A huge Auto Meter tach clearly shows the driver when to shift the transmission.

Skinny front wheels and custom headers are important for drag cars.

RUNNING GEAR
Steering: Recirculating ball
Front suspension: Double wishbones with coil springs and telescopic shock absorbers
Rear suspension: Live axle with upper and lower parallel links, coil springs and telescopic shock absorbers
Brakes: Discs (front and rear)
Wheels: Centerline, 15-in. dia.
Tires: BF Goodrich 15-in. dia. radials (front), Mickey Thompson 10 x 15-in. slicks (rear)

DIMENSIONS
Length: 155.5 in.   **Width:** 60.3 in.
Height: 61.3 in.   **Wheelbase:** 90.0 in.
Track: 54.0 in. (front), 45.7 in. (rear)
Weight: 1,870 lbs.

Ford COUPE

When Henry Ford launched America's first affordable V8 car, he could never have imagined that thousands of hot rodders would later choose it to modify into their dream machines.

"...it really takes off."

"This car's performance shouldn't be judged by its ancient appearance. Under the classic 1930s American coupe body, there is a 330-bhp small-block Chevy V8. It's not too highly stressed and idles quietly. With lots of low-down power, it can easily cope with modern traffic. If the road clears, though, and you floor the throttle, it really takes off. Its handling is is a little antiquated, but this car's Corvette rear end helps to keep things in line."

The tiny cockpit retains its 1930s look but has an extra touch of luxury.

Milestones

1932 Ford introduces America's first low-priced V8-engined car, ahead of arch-rival Chevrolet. Unfortunately, it is something of a rush job and early engine problems let Chevrolet take the production lead in 1933.

Henry Ford's "any color as long as it's black" quote doesn't apply to this Ford hot rod.

1934 The Ford range becomes totally V8-powered after all the four-cylinder models were dropped. They are speedy, simple and affordable cars, offered with a wide range of body styles.

The first V8 Ford hot rods were stripped down and mildly tuned.

1940s and 1950s As a cheap way of getting a performance car, young men start to modify 1930s V8 Fords starting the hot-rodding craze.

UNDER THE SKIN

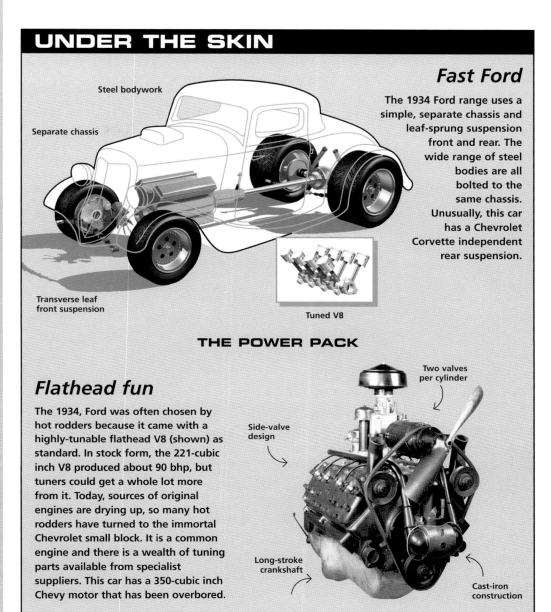

Steel bodywork

Separate chassis

Transverse leaf front suspension

Tuned V8

Fast Ford

The 1934 Ford range uses a simple, separate chassis and leaf-sprung suspension front and rear. The wide range of steel bodies are all bolted to the same chassis. Unusually, this car has a Chevrolet Corvette independent rear suspension.

THE POWER PACK

Flathead fun

The 1934, Ford was often chosen by hot rodders because it came with a highly-tunable flathead V8 (shown) as standard. In stock form, the 221-cubic inch V8 produced about 90 bhp, but tuners could get a whole lot more from it. Today, sources of original engines are drying up, so many hot rodders have turned to the immortal Chevrolet small block. It is a common engine and there is a wealth of tuning parts available from specialist suppliers. This car has a 350-cubic inch Chevy motor that has been overbored.

Two valves per cylinder

Side-valve design

Long-stroke crankshaft

Cast-iron construction

Classic custom

The 1934 Ford has always been a popular choice with hot rodders. At the start, it was just a case of stripping off all unnecessary components to reduce the weight and tuning up the flat-head V8. Nowadays, rodders are a little more sophisticated.

This customized full-fendered 1934 Ford retains its factory body panels.

Ford **COUPE**

Most stylish of the 1934 Ford model range, the V8 three-window Coupe turns even more heads today, especially when it looks as good as this hot rod.

Widened rear fenders

In order to cover the wider-than-stock rear tires, the fenders have been made larger by welding in a strip of steel.

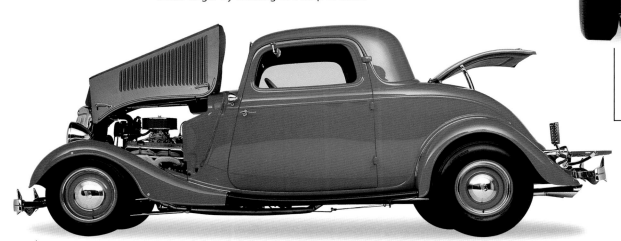

Nose-down, tail-up stance

The nose-down, tail-up stance clearly shows the Corvette-sourced rear suspension. It has been completely chromed to really show it off.

Simple front suspension

Like the Model T Ford, the 1934 car uses a transverse leaf-sprung solid front axle. Modern telescopic shocks help to keep it under control.

Corvette rear end

The original and simple leaf-sprung live rear axle has been replaced by a Corvette independent rear suspension with a single transverse leaf spring.

Chrome luggage rack

The chromed luggage rack is for show and is extremely unlikely to be used to carry any extra luggage.

Standard roof line

Many hot-rod Ford Coupes have a roof chop, in which the car's windshield pillars have been cut down by several inches to give the car a lower stance. This car has a standard roof line for a more classic look.

Filled roof

The original 1934 Fords had a fabric center roof section. This car has been modified with a custom welded sheet metal roof.

Skinny front tires

In traditional hot-rod style, the front tires are a lot narrower (6.5 inches) than those at the rear (8 inches).

Sprung bumpers

The 1930s equivalent of modern impact-absorbing bumpers are these stylish sprung-steel ones.

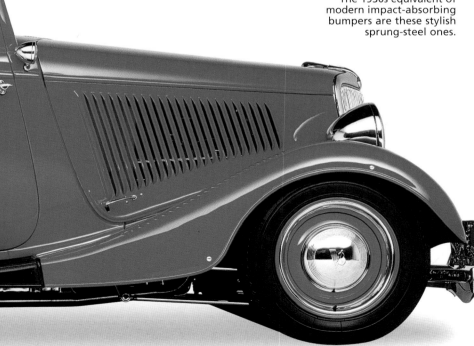

Specifications
1934 Ford Coupe

ENGINE

Type: Chevrolet V8

Construction: Cast-iron block and heads

Valve gear: Two valves per cylinder operated by a single camshaft via pushrods and rockers

Bore and stroke: 4.06 in. x 3.48 in.

Displacement: 358 c.i.

Compression ratio: 9.5:1

Induction system: Single four-barrel carburetor

Maximum power: 330 bhp at 5,500 rpm

Maximum torque: 339 lb-ft at 3,400 rpm

Top speed: 127 mph

0-60 mph: 8.7 sec.

TRANSMISSION

Four-speed manual

BODY/CHASSIS

Two-door coupe body on a separate steel chassis

SPECIAL FEATURES

To retain the classic hot-rod look, this car has standard-looking steel wheels rather than modern alloys.

The Chevrolet small-block V8 engine gives great performance. It has been overbored from 350 to 358 cubic inches.

RUNNING GEAR

Steering: Chevrolet Vega recirculating ball

Front suspension: Transverse leaf spring with telescopic shocks

Rear suspension: Corvette-sourced independent suspension with transverse leaf spring and telescopic shocks

Brakes: Discs (front), drums (rear)

Wheels: Pressed steel, 6.5 in. x 15 in. (front), 8 in. x 15 in. (rear)

Tires: 165/70 R15 (front), 205/60 R15 (rear)

DIMENSIONS

Length: 153 in.   **Width:** 65.9 in.

Height: 55.5 in.   **Wheelbase:** 102.5 in.

Track: 58.7 in. (front), 59.1 in. (rear)

Weight: 2,403 lbs.

Ford CRESTLINE SUNLINER

Although 1949-1951 Fords are often considered the classic post-war street machine, the later, more refined 1952-1954 Fords are also great for customizing. This period-looking 1952 Sunliner convertible complete with flames and a roof chop is a fine example.

"...glide by in style."

"Fuzzy dice and tuck 'n' roll upholstery were almost essential for a cruisin' custom back in the late 1950s. With a carbureted 302 small-block under the flamed hood, this classy custom can drive happily in modern traffic yet still offers plenty of old-fashioned torque. Power steering and brakes and a column-shifted automatic transmission make this Sunliner really easy to drive, giving you time to take in the stares of others as you glide by them in style."

Functional as well as tasteful, the white and black interior is almost timeless.

Milestones

1952 Squared-up styling

and a longer 115-inch wheelbase marks the new Ford line. Offered in Mainline, Customline and Crestline series, the latter includes a Sunliner convertible, Victoria hardtop and Country Squire wagon. The new cars prove to be a hit despite the ongoing Korean War; 671,733 Fords are built.

The basic design lasted through 1956—here is a Victoria glasstop.

1953 Ford celebrates

its golden anniversary and all models get special steering wheel medallions. A special 'Production Blitz' is intended to help steal sales from rival Chevrolet.

Fords were all-new in 1957 and were fitted with engines up to 312-cubic inches.

1954 A new Y-block, overhead-valve V8

replaces the venerable flathead. A new ball-joint front suspension also arrives.

UNDER THE SKIN

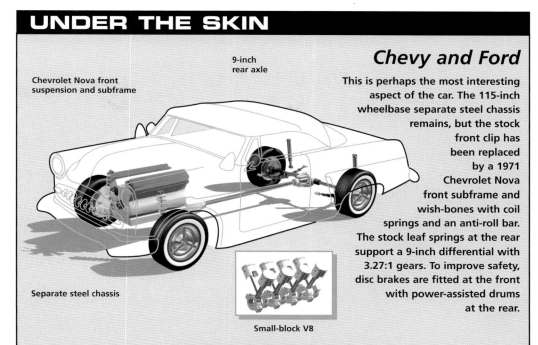

Chevrolet Nova front suspension and subframe

9-inch rear axle

Separate steel chassis

Small-block V8

Chevy and Ford

This is perhaps the most interesting aspect of the car. The 115-inch wheelbase separate steel chassis remains, but the stock front clip has been replaced by a 1971 Chevrolet Nova front subframe and wish-bones with coil springs and an anti-roll bar. The stock leaf springs at the rear support a 9-inch differential with 3.27:1 gears. To improve safety, disc brakes are fitted at the front with power-assisted drums at the rear.

THE POWER PACK

The mighty 302

Originally, this Sunliner had a Y-block 239 V8 under the hood packing 110 bhp. In the interest of better reliability, it has been replaced by a 302-cubic inch engine sourced from a 1972 Ford F-100 pickup. Introduced in 1968, the 302 is one of the most versatile Ford V8s. It has a reputation for being a torquey, tractable engine that easily responds to simple modifications. Retaining the stock, cast-iron intake and two-barrel Autolite carburetor, this engine puts out 150 bhp and 240 lb-ft of torque. This may not seem much on paper, but it is more than enough to make this custom a real mover.

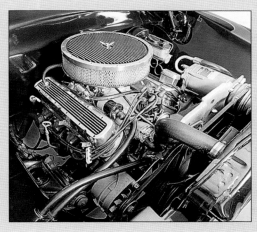

Still cool

It may be the earlier post-war Fords that are raved about by customizers, but the 1952-1954 models can be converted into rides that are just as cool. Some of the modifications on this car include a chopped carson top, flames and removed door handles.

Clever touches make this Sunliner really stand out.

Ford **CRESTLINE SUNLINER**

Flamed paint jobs are often depicted in contrasting hot/cold colors, but this Ford is ice-cool to the core, both inside and out. It puts a new face on the typical 1950s-style custom car.

Small-block V8

Replacing the less-than-satisfactory Y-block is a 1972 302-cubic inch V8. The small-block Windsor is often considered a latter-day flathead and a tuner's friend. In this application, it produces 150 bhp and 240 lb-ft of torque.

Toothy grill

One car that is notorious for its chromed tooth grill is the 1955 DeSoto. In keeping with its 1950s custom style, this Sunliner has a DeSoto grill mounted in place of the stock item.

C4 transmission

As it was conceived for cruising rather than all-out performance, this ride has a C4 three-speed automatic behind the engine. Despite its age, this unit boasts smoothness that some modern transmissions are hard pressed to match.

Radial tires

The tires on this car combine the safety of modern radials with the appearance of classic, wide, white bias-plys.

Tuck 'n' roll interior

Most customized cars of the late 1950s had tuck 'n' roll upholstery. Both the front and rear seats of this Sunliner are upholstered in this way, and the addition of fuzzy dice completes the period picture. An A/C system adds a touch of comfort for those hot summer nights.

Chopped windshield

The windshield has been dropped by three inches. The top is actually a Carson removable type rather than the normal folding power item.

Handmade taillights

The 1952 Fords marked the beginning of trade-mark circular taillights, but this one has custom, handformed lights.

Cool flames

The use of radiant 1990s colors like Jewel Green and black painted in the traditional 1950s-style flame pattern gives this Ford a classic, yet contemporary appearance.

1952 Ford Crestline Sunliner

ENGINE

Type: V8

Construction: Cast-iron block and heads

Valve gear: Two valves per cylinder operated by a single camshaft with pushrods and rockers

Bore and stroke: 4.0 in. x 3.0 in.

Displacement: 302 c.i.

Compression ratio: 8.5:1

Induction system: Autolite two-barrel carburetor

Maximum power: 150 bhp at 4,200 rpm

Maximum torque: 240 lb-ft at 3,100 rpm

Top speed: 112 mph

0-60 mph: 10.5 sec

TRANSMISSION

C4 three-speed automatic

BODY/CHASSIS

Separate steel chassis with two-door convertible body

SPECIAL FEATURES

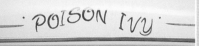

With its sharp green and black paint job, 'Poison Ivy' is an appropriate name.

Twin chrome spotlights were popular stock and custom accessories in the 1950s.

RUNNING GEAR

Steering: Recirculating ball

Front suspension: Unequal-length wishbones with coil springs, telescopic shock absorbers and anti-roll bar

Rear suspension: Live axle with leaf springs and telescopic shock absorbers

Brakes: Discs (front), drums (rear)

Wheels: Pressed steel, 14-in. dia.

Tires: Radial, 205/70 R14

DIMENSIONS

Length: 197.8 in. **Width:** 73.2 in.

Height: 56.8 in. **Wheelbase:** 115.0 in.

Track: 61.3 in. (front), 59.5 in. (rear)

Weight: 3,415 lbs.

Ford **DELUXE COUPE**

Fast, affordable and simple transportation—this was Henry Ford's motto through the mid-1940s. Today, these factors make cars like this Ford Deluxe Coupe equally appealing to the hot-rodding community.

"...lively acceleration."

"Despite what some people may say, there are few cars that share the beautiful rolling body lines of a 1940 Ford. On this particular example the interior has creature comforts which could only have been dreamed of five decades ago, like the velour upholstery, power windows and air-conditioning. A 350-cubic inch small-block Chevy V8 mated to a turbo 350 automatic transmission results in reliable and lively acceleration."

Grey velour upholstery and an aluminum dash keep the interior simple and tasteful.

Milestones

1937 A line of altered Fords with
a more pronounced grill and lights integrated into the bumpers are launched.

1938 A body revision including a new grill
and a reworked nose gives the Ford a fatter more rounded look.

Ford Deluxes got all-new styling for 1939. This model is a coupe.

1939 The Deluxe models are restyled again.
Fords finally receive hydraulic brakes and a column-mounted shifter instead of one mounted on the floor.

The 1940 Mercurys share a similar style with the Fords.

1940 Stylist Bob Gregorie alters the shape
again, which results in one of the prettiest and well balanced pre-war cars. Headlights are now sealed beam units and the trim is altered.

UNDER THE SKIN

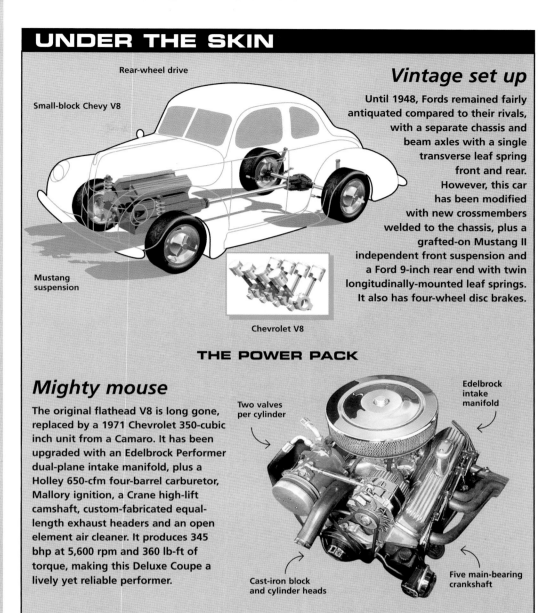

Rear-wheel drive

Small-block Chevy V8

Mustang suspension

Chevrolet V8

Vintage set up

Until 1948, Fords remained fairly antiquated compared to their rivals, with a separate chassis and beam axles with a single transverse leaf spring front and rear. However, this car has been modified with new crossmembers welded to the chassis, plus a grafted-on Mustang II independent front suspension and a Ford 9-inch rear end with twin longitudinally-mounted leaf springs. It also has four-wheel disc brakes.

THE POWER PACK

Mighty mouse

The original flathead V8 is long gone, replaced by a 1971 Chevrolet 350-cubic inch unit from a Camaro. It has been upgraded with an Edelbrock Performer dual-plane intake manifold, plus a Holley 650-cfm four-barrel carburetor, Mallory ignition, a Crane high-lift camshaft, custom-fabricated equal-length exhaust headers and an open element air cleaner. It produces 345 bhp at 5,600 rpm and 360 lb-ft of torque, making this Deluxe Coupe a lively yet reliable performer.

Two valves per cylinder

Edelbrock intake manifold

Cast-iron block and cylinder heads

Five main-bearing crankshaft

Firm favorite

Light weight, mechanical simplicity, an incredible supply of both stock and custom parts and an abundance of tuning shops ensure that 1940 model Fords will be cruising the drive-ins and tearing up the strips for many years to come.

Lowered and flamed, this Coupe sports the classic look.

Ford DELUXE COUPE

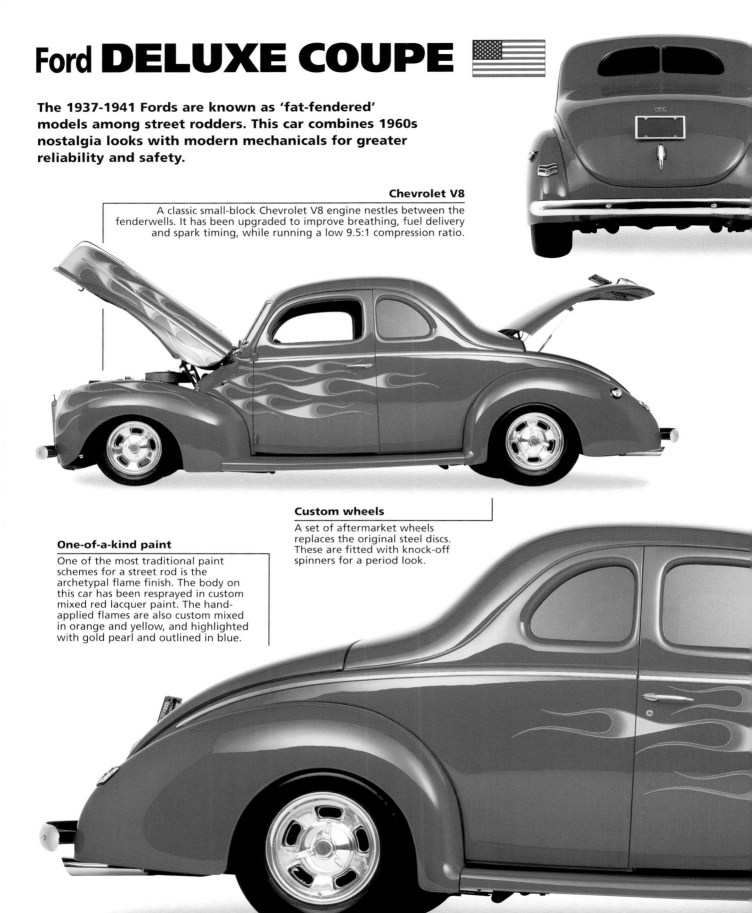

The 1937-1941 Fords are known as 'fat-fendered' models among street rodders. This car combines 1960s nostalgia looks with modern mechanicals for greater reliability and safety.

Chevrolet V8

A classic small-block Chevrolet V8 engine nestles between the fenderwells. It has been upgraded to improve breathing, fuel delivery and spark timing, while running a low 9.5:1 compression ratio.

Custom wheels

A set of aftermarket wheels replaces the original steel discs. These are fitted with knock-off spinners for a period look.

One-of-a-kind paint

One of the most traditional paint schemes for a street rod is the archetypal flame finish. The body on this car has been resprayed in custom mixed red lacquer paint. The hand-applied flames are also custom mixed in orange and yellow, and highlighted with gold pearl and outlined in blue.

GM transmission

The small-block V8 is backed up by a GM TurboHydramatic 350 automatic transmission. It benefits from a 2,200-rpm stall convertor for better torque multiplication off the line. The transmission is still column-shifted like the old Ford three-speed manual.

Lowered front suspension

In the interests of a lower sleeker look, the front suspension has been dropped several inches. It now includes a beam axle and transverse leaf spring, plus lever arm-type shock absorbers.

Luxury interior

Inside, this Deluxe has been totally reworked with a set of VDO aftermarket gauges in an aluminum instrument panel. It also has air-conditioning and power windows.

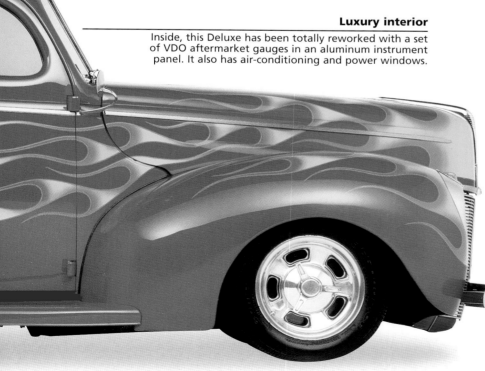

Specifications

1940 Ford Deluxe Coupe

ENGINE

Type: V8

Construction: Cast-iron block and heads

Valve gear: Two valves per cylinder operated by pushrods and rockers

Bore and stroke: 4.00 in. x 3.48 in.

Displacement: 350 c.i.

Compression ratio: 9.5:1

Induction system: Holley four-barrel carburetor

Maximum power: 345 bhp at 5,600 rpm

Maximum torque: 360 lb-ft at 4,000 rpm

Top speed: 123 mph

0-60 mph: 6.4 sec.

TRANSMISSION

GM TurboHydramatic 350 three-speed automatic

BODY/CHASSIS

Steel ladder-type chassis with two-door coupe body

SPECIAL FEATURES

1940 Ford Coupes can be distinguished from the 1939 models by their horizontal metal bars in the grill.

These alloy wheels are molded in the same style as vintage Halibrands.

RUNNING GEAR

Steering: Recirculating ball

Front suspension: Unequal length wishbones with coil springs and telescopic shock absorbers

Rear suspension: Live axle with transverse leaf spring

Brakes: Discs (front and rear)

Wheels: Magnesium, 7 x 14 in. (front), 8 x 15 in. (rear)

Tires: BF Goodrich Radial T/A

DIMENSIONS

Length: 179.0 in.   **Width:** 69.8 in.
Height: 58.8 in.   **Wheelbase:** 112.0 in.
Track: 58.0 in. (front), 56.0 in. (rear)
Weight: 2,769 lbs.

Ford FAIRLANE

Ford's 1957 line-up was widely regarded as one of Detroit's most stylish. The Fairlane 500 sat at the top of the regular Ford tree, helping the company to achieve one of its best sales years.

"...effortless pulling power."

"This car was produced before the great horsepower race in which Detroit later indulged. Still, for a 1957 car, this Fairlane goes pretty well thanks to its Thunderbird engine. The V8 is tuned for low-down torque rather than absolute power, which means lazy cruising and effortless pulling power. But when you want to move a little faster, the big 312-cubic inch V8 pulls its weight. It's no slowcoach, and can easily deal with modern traffic conditions."

Getting behind the wheel of this Fairlane is like stepping back in time.

Milestones

1957 Ford presents

its new line up including the 118-inch wheelbase Fairlane and the range-topping Fairlane 500. In mid-1957 a new Skyliner version is added with a retractable hardtop roof.

One of the most desirable body styles is the Fairlane convertible.

1958 A facelift

includes the addition of a Thunderbird-style bumper and grill, quad headlights and tail lights and a choice of two new FE-series V8 engines (332-cubic inch and 352-cubic inch). There is also the option of the new Cruise-O-Matic transmission.

The 1956 Fairlane had more rounded rear styling but a similar front end.

1959 A major reskin

revives a more simple style, with a sculpted V-shape back panel and low-level grill with star-like ornaments. A choice of new Galaxie models is also available.

UNDER THE SKIN

Dependable

Excitement was mostly cosmetic on 1950s cars. Under the skin, simplicity was the order of the day. It comes as no surprise to find a separate chassis, a leaf-spring suspension at the rear, an independent coil-spring front end and four-wheel drum brakes.

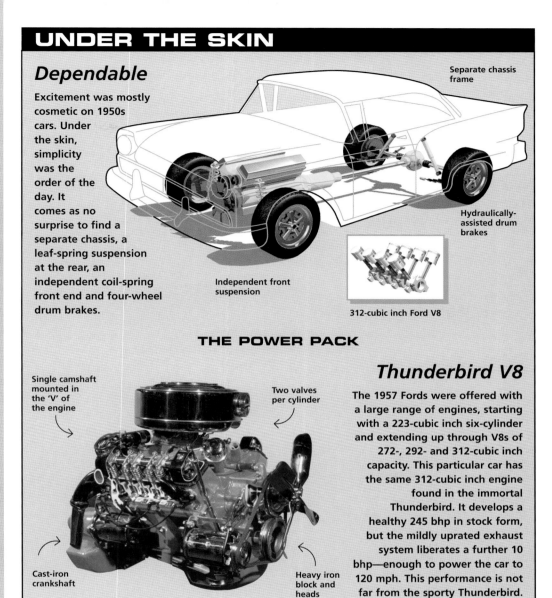

Separate chassis frame

Hydraulically-assisted drum brakes

Independent front suspension

312-cubic inch Ford V8

THE POWER PACK

Single camshaft mounted in the 'V' of the engine

Two valves per cylinder

Cast-iron crankshaft

Heavy iron block and heads

Thunderbird V8

The 1957 Fords were offered with a large range of engines, starting with a 223-cubic inch six-cylinder and extending up through V8s of 272-, 292- and 312-cubic inch capacity. This particular car has the same 312-cubic inch engine found in the immortal Thunderbird. It develops a healthy 245 bhp in stock form, but the mildly uprated exhaust system liberates a further 10 bhp—enough to power the car to 120 mph. This performance is not far from the sporty Thunderbird.

Range topper

The 1957 Ford range began with the entry-level, sub-$2,000 Custom and spanned up to the Fairlane 500 Club Victoria and Skyliner with a retractable hardtop at the top end. Ford offered the cars with a 144 bhp six cylinder to a 240 bhp supercharged V8.

The Fairlane hardtop coupe is one of the best-looking of the 1957 range.

Ford **FAIRLANE**

The 1957 Fairlane boasts tasteful styling for the period—a factor in its favor nowadays. This one has been subtly modified to retain that classic look.

Modern paint

The body of this restored and customized car has been resprayed in yellow and white acrylic paint.

Thunderbird engine

The base engine for the 1957 Fairlane was a modest six-cylinder. This car has received a useful increase in power by fitting a 255-bhp Thunderbird V8.

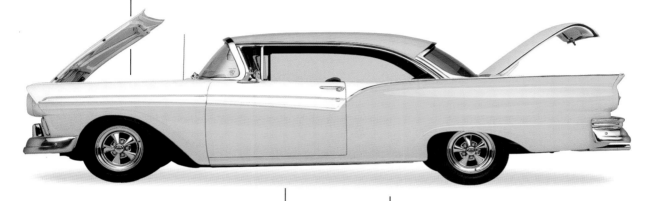

Automatic transmission

The Ford-O-Matic three-speed automatic transmission was optional on 1957 models and provides easy gear shifts.

Custom trim

The upholstery is black and charcoal velour, with yellow piping on the seats and rear package tray. Other additions include Auto Meter gauges, air-conditioning, and a powerful stereo.

Safety interior

Ford began its safety drive in 1956. This car is fitted with a dished steering wheel, padded dash, break-away rear-view mirror, and crash-proof door locks.

Partial dechroming
In order to give this car clean and uncluttered lines, much of the chrome trim has been removed.

Classic styling
Unlike the gaudy and contrived excesses of some late-1950s cars, the Fairlane was quite simple and understated.

Specifications

1957 Ford Fairlane 500

ENGINE

Type: V8

Construction: Cast-iron cylinder block and cylinder heads

Valve gear: Two valves per cylinder operated by a single camshaft

Bore and stroke: 3.90 in. x 3.44 in.

Displacement: 312 c.i.

Compression ratio: 9.7:1

Induction system: Single Holley carburetor

Maximum power: 255 bhp at 4,600 rpm

Maximum torque: 354 lb-ft at 2,800 rpm

Top speed: 120 mph

0-60 mph: 10.2 sec.

TRANSMISSION

Ford-O-Matic three-speed automatic

BODY/CHASSIS

Separate chassis with steel two-door coupe bodywork

SPECIAL FEATURES

In 1957, the Fairlane had single rear lights; twin lights were fitted in 1958.

Chrome valve covers and air cleaner, and headers liven up the T-bird V8.

RUNNING GEAR

Steering: Recirculating ball

Front suspension: Independent with coil springs and telescopic shocks

Rear suspension: Rigid axle with leaf springs and telescopic shocks

Brakes: Four-wheel drums

Wheels: Cragar, 15-in. dia.

Tires: 235/60 x 15 in.

DIMENSIONS

Length: 207.5 in.　　**Width:** 77 in.

Height: 56.5 in.　　**Wheelbase:** 118 in.

Track: 59 in. (front), 56.4 in. (rear)

Weight: 3,400 lbs.

Ford FALCON

Super Gas is one of the toughest categories in NHRA drag racing, and most competitors run Chevy-powered vehicles. It is not so with this Falcon, which screams down the ¼-mile with Ford's finest under the hood.

"...breathtaking experience."

"Power and speed are everything at this level of NHRA racing, and one drive in this Falcon will show you that this little car delivers a lot of both. Strap yourself securely into the lightweight bucket seat, switch on the fuel pump and flip the starter switch. With around 700 bhp, the driving experience is breathtaking. Once you hit the gas, all you can do is just sit there and hold on as the car starts up and then rockets down the strip covering the ¼-mile in less than 10 seconds."

A custom-built interior houses a pair of lightweight buckets and a B&M shifter.

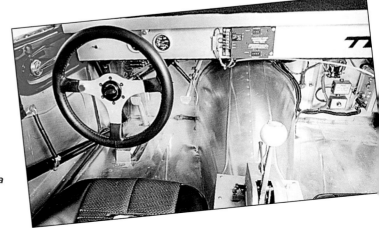

Milestones

1960 Ford launches its compact

Falcon, an utterly conventional car offered in two- and four-door sedan forms or as a station wagon. A 144-c.i. inline six is the only engine available. In its debut year an incredible 435,676 are built.

Sprints finally got a V8 in 1963, in keeping with their sporty nature.

1961 A bigger, 170-c.i. six

becomes available and a Futura coupe (with bucket seats) is added to the range, in an attempt to add sportiness. Falcon output this year numbers 474,191 units.

1965 was the last year for sprints and convertibles.

1963 The Futura becomes

a separate series and a convertible is added to the range. A 260-c.i. V8 is also made available in the Futura this year. A redesigned Falcon arrives for the 1964 model year.

UNDER THE SKIN

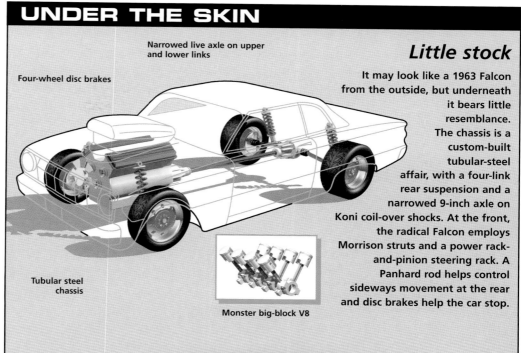

Four-wheel disc brakes

Narrowed live axle on upper and lower links

Tubular steel chassis

Monster big-block V8

Little stock

It may look like a 1963 Falcon from the outside, but underneath it bears little resemblance. The chassis is a custom-built tubular-steel affair, with a four-link rear suspension and a narrowed 9-inch axle on Koni coil-over shocks. At the front, the radical Falcon employs Morrison struts and a power rack-and-pinion steering rack. A Panhard rod helps control sideways movement at the rear and disc brakes help the car stop.

THE POWER PACK

Simply overkill

With 164 bhp from its 260 V8, the 1963 Falcon Futura Sprint was quite a peppy little mover in its day, but this one gets its motivation from something bigger. Sitting in the custom-built chassis is a huge 460 V8 (Ford's largest production passenger car engine). It has been bored and stroked and has steel Manley Chevy rods pinned to Probe 13.5:1-compression pistons. It has a solid-lifter Crane camshaft that opens and closes the valves in a pair of ported and polished J. Bittle heads. Up top there's a Ford Performance aluminum intake manifold and a monster 1050-cfm Holley Dominator carburetor.

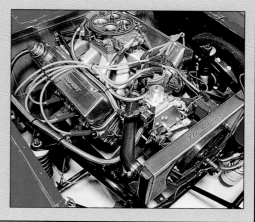

Sprinter

If you ask any Falcon aficionado which would be the best pick, a 289-poweredSprint convertible from 1964-1965 would be it. The earlier cars are great machines; simple, plentiful and relatively easy to build into a killer street or strip warrior.

Falcons are quite rare in Southern California Super Gas events.

Ford **FALCON**

It may resemble a 1963 Falcon, but this car is almost totally custom fabricated. Perhaps the most interesting thing about it is that the shell is actually from a convertible, with a hardtop from another Falcon grafted on.

Lightweight bumpers

Shaving as many pounds as possible was of primary concern when building this car. That approach extends to the bumpers, which are fiberglass items and have been sectioned to make them fit as close to the body as possible.

Killer V8

With a genuine 500 cubic inches and a huge 1050-cfm carburetor, this engine makes a tremendous amount of horsepower, more than 700, in fact. This enables the bantam weight Falcon to scream down the quarter-mile in just 9.2 seconds.

Strut front suspension

Stock Falcons came with a short-long-arm front suspension and coil-over shocks, but both the stock chassis and IFS have been replaced by a pair of Morrison struts. In the interest of weight transfer, the anti-roll bar has been omitted and lightweight wheels, with skinnies, have been fitted.

Custom interior

A whole new interior has been fabricated from aluminum sheeting, including the dash and the transmission tunnel (on which sits a B&M shifter for the Powerglide transmission). Safety is courtesy of a roll cage and Simpson twin harnesses.

Free-flowing exhaust

To expel the spent gases as quickly as possible, the big motor has a pair of Hooker 2½-inch diameter headers bolted to it. Besides getting rid of the spent gases, they help the engine make a truly thunderous trip down the strip.

Specifications

1963 Ford Falcon Sprint

ENGINE
Type: V8

Construction: Cast-iron block with alloy heads

Valve gear: Two valves per cylinder operated by a single V-mounted camshaft with pushrods and rockers

Bore and stroke: 4.39 in. x 4.125 in.

Displacement: 500 c.i.

Compression ratio: 13.5:1

Induction system: Holley Dominator 1050-cfm four-barrel carburetor

Maximum power: 710 bhp at 7,000 rpm

Maximum torque: 685 lb-ft at 5,200 rpm

Top speed: 230 mph

0-60 mph: 2.8 sec.

TRANSMISSION
Powerglide two-speed automatic

BODY/CHASSIS
Tubular-steel chassis with two-door hardtop body

SPECIAL FEATURES

Lexan glass is used for all windows to save as much weight as possible.

Wheelie bars help keep the car straight off the tee.

RUNNING GEAR
Steering: Rack-and-pinion

Front suspension: Morrison struts, lower control arms and telescopic shock absorbers

Rear suspension: Live axle, four-bar links, coil springs, telescopic shock absorbers and Panhard rod

Brakes: Discs (front and rear)

Wheels: Centerline lightweight

Tires: BFGoodrich radial T/A (front), Goodyear Drag Slicks (rear)

DIMENSIONS
Length: 183.7 in. **Width:** 70.8 in.

Height: 51.5 in. **Wheelbase:** 109.5 in.

Track: 56.9 in. (front), 48.5 in. (rear)

Weight: 2,015 lbs.

Ford GALAXIE

Ford Galaxie Starliners are powerful even in stock form. This particular model has been fitted with a variety of vintage Ford high performance running gear such as the infamous, ultra-rare, marginally street legal 427 SOHC.

"...prowess of performance."

"No matter what car you put the outlawed-by-NASCAR 427 SOHC engine in, it is guaranteed to give it an extraordinary prowess of performance. The only factor that keeps this Starliner from dropping its 0-60 mph elapsed time is the tires. Complimenting the hand-built 625-bhp engine is perhaps Ford's finest driveline. It includes a Top-Loader' 4-speed and a 9-inch rear that houses 4.30:1 gears. Though it's far from original, this street machine was sure done right."

Drop the pedal and hang on! Soon everything outside the windshield becomes a blur.

Milestones

1960 Ford introduces
a new full-size hardtop line, and a new Starliner fastback hardtop joins the Galaxie series. It is conceived to reduce aerodynamic drag on NASCAR tracks and helps Ford to win the championship this year.

For 1960 the full-size Fords were completely revised.

1961 The Starliner
returns, although full-size Fords are reduced by four inches in length and two in width. The FE series 352-cubic inch engine is stroked to 390 and the most powerful version produces 375 bhp at 6,000 rpm. Only 29,669 Starliners are built this year and poor sales ensure that it does not return for 1962.

Like their GM rivals, Ford 'biggies' had shorter and narrower bodies in 1961.

1965 A restyled
full-size Ford, with all-coil suspension, goes on sale. A single overhead-cam version of the 427 is made available to racers.

UNDER THE SKIN

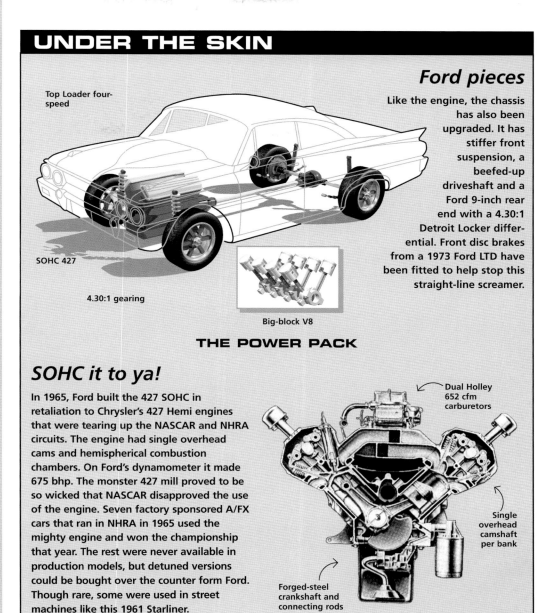

Top Loader four-speed

SOHC 427

4.30:1 gearing

Big-block V8

THE POWER PACK

Ford pieces

Like the engine, the chassis has also been upgraded. It has stiffer front suspension, a beefed-up driveshaft and a Ford 9-inch rear end with a 4.30:1 Detroit Locker differential. Front disc brakes from a 1973 Ford LTD have been fitted to help stop this straight-line screamer.

SOHC it to ya!

In 1965, Ford built the 427 SOHC in retaliation to Chrysler's 427 Hemi engines that were tearing up the NASCAR and NHRA circuits. The engine had single overhead cams and hemispherical combustion chambers. On Ford's dynamometer it made 675 bhp. The monster 427 mill proved to be so wicked that NASCAR disapproved the use of the engine. Seven factory sponsored A/FX cars that ran in NHRA in 1965 used the mighty engine and won the championship that year. The rest were never available in production models, but detuned versions could be bought over the counter form Ford. Though rare, some were used in street machines like this 1961 Starliner.

Dual Holley 652 cfm carburetors

Single overhead camshaft per bank

Forged-steel crankshaft and connecting rods

Fastback style

The Galaxie Starliner arrived in 1960—its main purpose was to keep Ford competitive in NASCAR. In its day the Starliner was one of the best-looking Fords. Today its fastback design and low stance makes it a natural to be transformed into a street machine.

The Starliner debuted in 1960 but only lasted until the following year.

Ford GALAXIE

The 427 SOHC engines were never installed in any production cars. Although the handful that were offered were scoffed up by racers and hot rodders alike nearly as soon as they were available in 1965, their status is still legendary today.

Ultra-rare engine

Originally fitted with a 390, the owner of this car has installed a 427-cubic inch single overhead cam engine. This very rare power unit was developed by Ford to compete with the hemi Chryslers in NASCAR and NHRA sanctioned racing.

Manual transmission

Most Starliners are equipped with C6 automatics, but this one has a Borg-Warner T-10. To cope with the torque of the big V8, it has a heavy-duty clutch linkage.

Fastback styling

The fastback roof not only looks good, but it had a purpose. In 1961 Ford designed this car to be as aerodynamic as possible for specially prepared cars that raced in NASCAR. This was done to help reduce high speed aerodynamic drag.

Custom exhaust headers

For less restricted exhaust flow, the stock manifolds have been replaced by custom-fabricated tubular units. Doug Thorley was one of the largest suppliers of headers to drag racers in the 1960s.

Teardrop hood

Because the engine's induction system used a high rise intake manifold and dual carburetors, extra clearance was necessary. This stylish 'teardrop' shaped scoop was molded to a fiberglass hood to give the engine the space it required. Another added benefit was the two openings at the cowl that allowed hot air from the engine to escape. This hood style was immortalized in the 1964 lightweight Galaxie and Thunderbolt factory race cars. It quickly became a popular add-on for many other Ford models.

Full interior

As it is a street machine rather than a factory drag racer, this Galaxie still has a full stock interior and two-tone upholstery.

Specifications
1961 Ford Galaxie Starliner

ENGINE

Type: V8

Construction: Cast-iron block and heads

Valve gear: Two valves per cylinder operated by a single overhead camshaft per bank via rockers

Bore and stroke: 4.23 in. x 3.78 in.

Displacement: 427 c.i.

Compression ratio: 12.5:1

Induction system: Twin Holley four-barrel carburetors

Maximum power: 625 bhp at 7,000 rpm

Maximum torque: 515 lb-ft at 3,800 rpm

Top speed: 130 mph

0-60 mph: 5.4 sec.

TRANSMISSION

Borg-Warner 'Top-Loader' T-10 four-speed

BODY/CHASSIS

Perimeter steel chassis with two-door steel hardtop body

SPECIAL FEATURES

Starliner emblems garnish the rear quarter panels.

Round tail lights and a simulated grill treatment on the rear valance are hallmarks of early 1960s Fords.

RUNNING GEAR

Steering: Recirculating ball

Front suspension: Unequal length wishbones with coil springs and telescopic shock absorbers

Rear suspension: Live rear axle with semi-elliptic leaf springs and telescopic shock absorbers

Brakes: Drums (front and rear)

Wheels: Torque Thrust magnesium, 15-in. dia.

Tires: BFG radials

DIMENSIONS

Length: 463.0 in.   **Width:** 190.0 in.

Height: 124.0 in.   **Wheelbase:** 119.0 in.

Track: 145.0 in. (front), 136.0 in. (rear)

Weight: 3,660 lbs.

Ford MODEL 18 COUPE

Other Deuce hot rods may be quicker, better-finished or more extravagant, but few can match this Chrome Yellow, five-window Ford Model 18 Coupe, which was one of the star attractions in the movie *American Graffiti*.

"...remarkably nostalgic."

"One thing that becomes really apparent after driving this car is how remarkably nostalgic it feels by modern standards. The 327 V8 engine coupled to a four-speed manual transmission gives the car excellent acceleration. With its four Rochester two-barrel carburetors atop a Man-a-fre intake manifold, the V8 has instant power on demand at any rpm. Like most 1930s street rods of the day this one has been stripped of its hood panels, fenders and floorboards."

Black tuck 'n' roll upholstery and a four speed shifter take you back to the 1960s.

Milestones

1932 Replacing the 1928-vintage Model

A are two new Fords—a four-cylinder Model B and V8-engined Model 18—marking the first time a performance automobile is available in the U.S. V8s outsell the four-cylinder cars by a considerable margin.

John Milner, played by actor Paul LeMat, gets harassed by local law enforcement in the movie American Graffiti.

1972 Young film maker

George Lucas begins work on one of his earlier films: *American Graffiti*. It is a coming-of-age movie set around the California street scene, circa 1962. One of the featured vehicles is this 1932 Ford Coupe.

Also from the movie, fellow street racer Bob Falfa, played by a young Harrison Ford, challenges Milner to a race.

1998 *American Graffiti is* re-released,

25 years after its debut, with additional footage.

UNDER THE SKIN

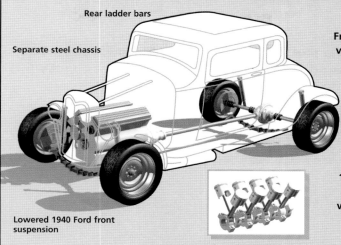

Rear ladder bars

Separate steel chassis

Lowered 1940 Ford front suspension

Chevrolet small-block V8

Classic hot rod

From the factory, 1932 Fords were very basic cars, with a simple, yet strong ladder-type separate chassis and beam axles front and rear, suspended by transverse leaf springs. The Milner Coupe retains the stock front suspension but has lower A-arms and has been dropped. At the rear is a Chevy 10-bolt rear axle, also suspended by a transverse leaf spring, but with a pair of ladder bars to help traction. Braking is provided by 1940 Ford drums.

THE POWER PACK

1960s vintage

With the introduction of the Chevrolet small-block V8 in 1955, rodders had a new low-cost powerplant, which was ideally suited to their pre-war cars. This 32 Ford Coupe is powered by a 1966-vintage, 327-cubic inch, small-block V8—the same engine from when George Lucas first discovered the car. It is stock, except for "Fuelie" cylinder heads, a Man-a-fre, dual-plane, cast-iron intake manifold and four GM Rochester two-barrel carburetors, controlled by a non progressive throttle linkage. These few alterations enable the mighty mouse motor to kick out 370 bhp at 6,000 rpm.

Rolling nostalgia

An almost perfect recreation of an early-1960s-style hot rod, this 1932 5-window coupe has all the classic street rod features—ladder bars, chrome reverse wheels, exposed engine, exhaust headers, multiple carburetors and a loud paint job. Even today, this rolling piece of movie history never fails to draw a crowd.

This famous 5-window coupe has spawned many replicas.

Ford MODEL 18 COUPE

A rolling piece of nostalgia and movie history, this famous yellow five-window Coupe still draws admiring glances wherever it goes, and will no doubt continue to do so for many years to come.

Classic V8 engine

Nestling between the framerails of this nostalgic rod is a 1966 327-cubic inch Chevrolet small-block, perhaps the most popular mill used by hot rodders during the early and mid-1960s. With its Fuelie heads and four Rochester two-barrel carburetors, it puts out 370 bhp.

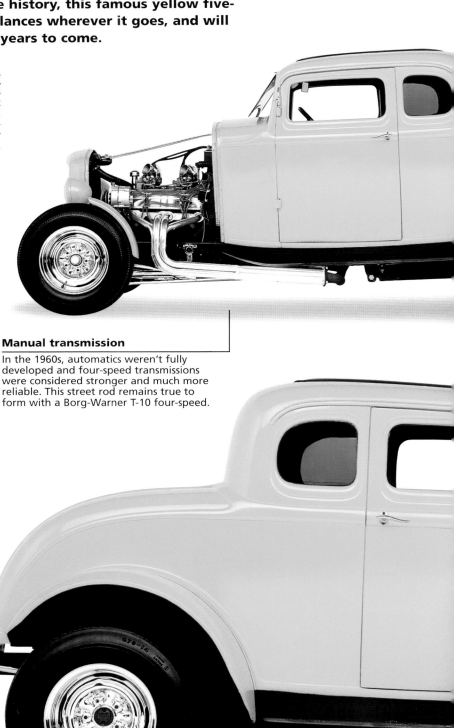

Manual transmission

In the 1960s, automatics weren't fully developed and four-speed transmissions were considered stronger and much more reliable. This street rod remains true to form with a Borg-Warner T-10 four-speed.

Ladder bars

Traction is a problem on light, high horsepower machines. To improve bite off the line, many owners install ladder bars on the rear axle.

Chevy rear end

For those thrill-seekers who wanted reliable performance in the late 1950s and 1960s, Chevy parts were among the strongest, least expensive, and the most abundant around. The infamous 10-bolt rear is found under many hot rods, including this one.

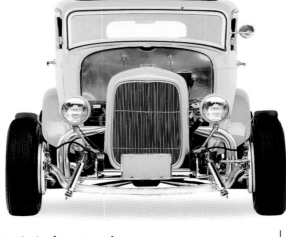

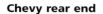

Almost stock suspension

Amazingly, this rod has a stock 1932 Ford front axle, which has been lowered to give a raked appearance. It is still suspended by a transverse leaf spring, but lower A-arms help improve the ride slightly.

Exhaust headers

Many of the classic hot rods are loud, and proud. This car originally had open exhaust headers, but a full exhaust has been added to keep noise levels down.

Specifications

1932 Ford Model 18 Coupe

ENGINE

Type: V8

Construction: Cast-iron block and heads

Valve gear: Two valves per cylinder operated by a single V-mounted camshaft with pushrods and rockers

Bore and stroke: 4.00 in. x 3.25 in.

Displacement: 327 c.i.

Compression ratio: 11.0:1

Induction system: Four Rochester two-barrel carburetors

Maximum power: 370 bhp at 6,000 rpm

Maximum torque: 380 lb-ft at 3,800 rpm

Top speed: 125 mph

0-60 mph: 6.2 sec.

TRANSMISSION

Borg-Warner T-10 four-speed manual

BODY/CHASSIS

Separate steel chassis with steel five-window coupe body

SPECIAL FEATURES

Chromed full-length exhaust headers were a common fitment to 1960s rods.

The Borg-Warner T-10 four-speed transmission features a Hurst shifter topped by a piston shift knob.

RUNNING GEAR

Steering: Recirculating-ball

Front suspension: Beam axle with transverse leaf spring, lower A-arms and telescopic shock absorbers

Rear suspension: Live axle with transverse leaf spring, ladder bars and telescopic shock absorbers

Brakes: Drums (front and rear)

Wheels: Genie chrome reverse

Tires: E-78 14 (front), G-78 14 (rear)

DIMENSIONS

Length: 136.1 in.   **Width:** 74.7 in.

Height: 62.1 in.   **Wheelbase:** 106.5 in.

Track: 67.9 in. (front), 66.9 in. (rear)

Weight: 2,680 lbs.

Ford Model 81A

By the early 1930s, Ford had been demoted to number two in the U.S. market by Chevrolet. In order to rectify the balance, a low-cost V8 engine was developed and with it came a whole new generation of hot-rodding.

"...head-turning looks."

"The luxuriously upholstered cabin is a million miles away from the sparse demeanor of the original 1938 Model 81A DeLuxe. And the difference becomes more apparent when the small-block Chevy V8 is fired up. The lightweight body and highly tuned engine combine to produce phenomenal acceleration, and the Mustang front suspension provides good high-speed stability. With its head-turning looks and fantastic engine, there is only one thing to do cruise."

Customization in this case means a wood dashboard, Ford SVO gauges and air conditioning.

Milestones

1932 In order to regain
the top spot from Chevrolet, Ford releases the first low-priced V8-engined car in the U.S. Plans for a radical X8 are dropped because of logistical problems.

1937 Fords are popular for fat-fendered customization.

1934 Having overcome
customer resistance, the whole Ford range is offered with V8s. With new carburetors, power rises to 85 bhp.

The 1940 model was one of the most classically designed Fords.

1938 Standard and DeLuxe
models are given separate identities having previously signified equipment differences. They are available in numerous styles.

1940s After the end of World War II,
there is an explosion in the popularity of hot-rodding. The craze continues into the 1960s and still has a substantial following today.

UNDER THE SKIN

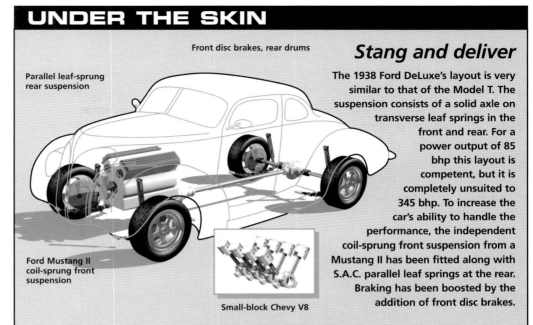

Front disc brakes, rear drums

Parallel leaf-sprung rear suspension

Ford Mustang II coil-sprung front suspension

Small-block Chevy V8

Stang and deliver

The 1938 Ford DeLuxe's layout is very similar to that of the Model T. The suspension consists of a solid axle on transverse leaf springs in the front and rear. For a power output of 85 bhp this layout is competent, but it is completely unsuited to 345 bhp. To increase the car's ability to handle the performance, the independent coil-sprung front suspension from a Mustang II has been fitted along with S.A.C. parallel leaf springs at the rear. Braking has been boosted by the addition of front disc brakes.

THE POWER PACK

Chevy small-block

Although the original Ford 221-cubic inch V8 is a classic power supply, the bulletproof Chevrolet 350-cubic inch motor has been fitted. The small-block Chevy offers a high degree of flexibility, unmatched availability of parts and sufficient performance potential to satisfy any serious rodder. In order to boost performance, an Edelbrock four-barrel carburetor has been fitted, along with an MSD electronic ignition. Although the compression ratio is a relatively low 9.5:1, the engine still packs plenty of power. It produces 345 bhp at 5,600 rpm and 360 lb-ft of torque at 4,000 rpm.

Rodders

In the late 1930s, cars receive a semi-streamlined look. For 1938, Ford gave the 81A range separate looks from the Standard and DeLuxe models. The two-door coupe versions are much more attractive with their sweeping curves, which naturally lend themselves to unusual paint schemes.

The individuality of a hot rod encapsulates the character of the owner.

Ford **MODEL 81A**

Hot-rodding is a labor of love. The time and effort required to turn a humble 1938 Ford into a refined highway cruiser is beyond the reach of most people. However, the outcome—a truly unique car—is worth it.

Chevrolet small-block V8

The 350-cubic inch Chevrolet engine has been modified for optimum street performance. The addition of an Edelbrock four-barrel carburetor and performance engine tuning has increased the power output to 345 bhp.

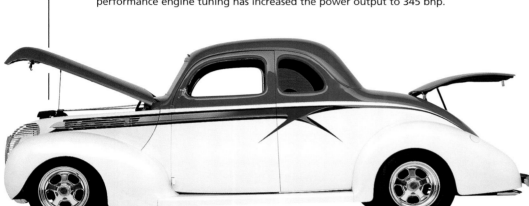

DeLuxe grill

The simplest way of distinguishing the 1938 DeLuxe and Standard models is the front grill. On DeLuxe versions, the top is sculpted into two pronounced arcs, whereas the grill on the Standard car has a horizontal top.

Mustang front suspension

The lowered front suspension is taken from the Ford Mustang II. The independent arrangement with coil springs and telescopic shocks offers more stability and greater comfort than the stock solid axle.

Outlandish color scheme

To augment the car's styling, this rod is painted pink over white with customized graphics consisting of a pearl-foil blue stripe with candy silver, purple, gray, burgundy and gold.

Luxurious interior

One of the great things about building your own car is being able to add the fittings that you want. This car has a natural-wood dash with Ford SVO gauges, burgundy and mauve pleated door and seat panels, air conditioning and a CD player.

Modern disc brakes

Braking is one area where big advances in technology have been made since the 1930s. Brakes from that era often lack bite and feel. To cope with the extra performance, this car has been fitted with front disc brakes.

Specifications

1938 Ford Model 81A DeLuxe Coupe

ENGINE
Type: V8

Construction: Cast-iron block and heads

Valve gear: Two valves per cylinder operated by a single camshaft with pushrods and rockers

Bore and stroke: 4.00 in. x 3.48 in.

Displacement: 350 c.i.

Compression ratio: 9.5:1

Induction system: Single four-barrel carburetor

Maximum power: 345 bhp at 5,600 rpm

Maximum torque: 360 lb-ft at 4,000 rpm

Top speed: 122 mph

0-60 mph: 6.1 sec.

TRANSMISSION
Four-speed automatic

BODY/CHASSIS
Separate steel chassis with two-door coupe body

SPECIAL FEATURES

To complete the slick customized look, 15-inch alloy wheels have been fitted.

The billet side mirrors follow the "streamlined appearance" theme.

RUNNING GEAR
Steering: Recirculating-ball

Front suspension: Independent with coil springs and telescopic shock absorbers

Rear suspension: Parallel leaf springs, live axle with telescopic shock absorbers

Brakes: Discs (front), drums (rear)

Wheels: Aluminum, 15 x 6 in. (front), 15 x 8 in. (rear)

Tires: 165/40-15 (front), 205/60-15 (rear)

DIMENSIONS
Length: 155.3 in.   **Width:** 71.3 in.

Height: 62.4 in.   **Wheelbase:** 112.0 in.

Track: 56.9 in. (front), 59.0 in. (rear)

Weight: 2,350 lbs.

Ford MODEL A

Although many customizers prefer the body lines of the 1932 Ford three-window coupe, the owner of this car decided to go for something different by selecting a 1930 Model A pickup truck.

"...grips the asphalt."

"Sliding behind the wheel, the driver is greeted by a sparse, color-coded dash—a reminder of how far technology has come since the 1930s. The seats, however, offer excellent lateral support. Turn the key and the distinctive sound of a Ford 351-cubic inch V8 rumbles to life. With 304 bhp and low weight, acceleration is brisk, yet the fun does not stop there. With modern 60 series rubber and uprated suspension, this Model A firmly grips the asphalt."

The cabin is decidedly retro with its sparse dash and low-back b ucket seats.

Milestones

1928 After producing
15 million units, the Model T is finally retired. Its replacement, the Model A, has a 40 bhp four-cylinder engine and conventional transmission. The Model A is produced both in the U.S. and U.K.

The Model A pickup was a reliable and affordable work horse.

1930 Despite the
financial troubles of the Depression, the Model A remains popular and Ford manages to sell 1.1 million examples—almost twice as many as arch rival Chevrolet.

Shown in this photo is the three generations of the Ford family.

1932 Ford decide to replace
the Model A with a much improved car, the Model B. Powered by a new V8 engine, it has outstanding performance for such a low-priced car, though engineering problems with the Model B enable Chevrolet to build more cars this year.

UNDER THE SKIN

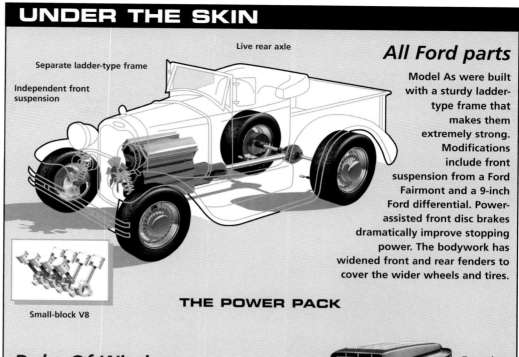

Live rear axle

Separate ladder-type frame

Independent front suspension

Small-block V8

All Ford parts

Model As were built with a sturdy ladder-type frame that makes them extremely strong. Modifications include front suspension from a Ford Fairmont and a 9-inch Ford differential. Power-assisted front disc brakes dramatically improve stopping power. The bodywork has widened front and rear fenders to cover the wider wheels and tires.

THE POWER PACK

Duke Of Windsor

Most rodders choose to power their vehicles with the ubiquitous small-block Chevy. This one, however, features a 351-cubic inch Ford Windsor V8. It has been lightly massaged with freer-flowing exhaust headers, an Edelbrock intake manifold and a Holley four-barrel carburetor and a slightly higher-lift camshaft. These modifications bump power output up to a solid 304 bhp, yet the tuning is mild enough to allow this car to be used as a daily driver.

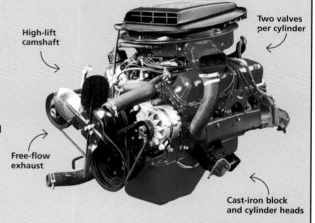

High-lift camshaft

Two valves per cylinder

Free-flow exhaust

Cast-iron block and cylinder heads

Popularity

Fords from the 1930s are very popular to customize into a hot rod or street machine. This Model A, with a small bed and convertible roof, has style and practicality. The 351 cubic inch Ford Windsor V8-powered Model A pickup makes for one terrific daily driver and practical parts hauler.

This one-of-a-kind Model A is driven daily.

Ford **MODEL A**

With its classic styling, reliable V8 engine, and modern suspension, this Model A pickup fills the dual role of showpiece and daily driver remarkably well.

Convertible roof
A Model A roadster donated its convertible top mechanism. The top itself is trimmed in high-quality European tan cloth.

Ford V8 engine
Unlike many other street rods, this one has a Ford small-block V8 engine, which has been mildly worked to produce 304 bhp.

Siren
A truly unique touch is a siren, taken from an original Model A Fire Chief's vehicle. The Model A was common choice for fire and police services.

Updated front suspension
A complete front suspension assembly from a 1979 Fairmont provides a smooth ride and improves handling. McPherson struts and coil springs replace the original beam axle and transverse leaf spring.

Automatic transmission
A bulletproof Ford C4 automatic makes light work of everyday driving and enables smooth gearchanges and greater reliability.

Power brakes
For safe braking, large-diameter front discs and rear drums were sourced from a 1984 Mustang. The system is servo-assisted for less pedal effort.

Reworked fenders

Not noticeable at first glance, the fenders are actually taken from a 1929 Model A and have been reshaped to match the lines of a 1930 model. They are wider to cover the larger wheels and tires.

Opening windshield

To give even more cabin ventilation, the windshield is hinged and can open outward.

Specifications

1930 Ford Model A

ENGINE

Type: V8

Construction: Cast-iron block and heads

Valve gear: Two valves per cylinder operated by pushrods and rockers

Bore and stroke: 4 in. x 3.5 in.

Displacement: 351 c.i.

Compression ratio: 9.5:1

Induction system: Single Holley 700 cfm four-barrel carburetor

Maximum power: 304 bhp at 4,900 rpm

Maximum torque: 380 lb-ft at 3,200

Top speed: 129 mph

0-60 mph: 5.3 sec.

TRANSMISSION

Ford C4 three-speed automatic

BODY/CHASSIS

Separate chassis with steel pickup body

SPECIAL FEATURES

Free standing headlights and externally mounted horn add a period touch to this unique street rod.

For weekend trips a matching trailer can be hitched behind this pickup.

RUNNING GEAR

Steering: Power-assisted, recirculating ball

Front suspension: McPherson struts with coil springs, telescopic shocks and an anti-roll bar

Rear suspension: Live rear axle suspended by leaf springs and telescopic shocks

Brakes: Servo assisted discs 11-in. dia. (front), drums 9.5-in. dia. (rear)

Wheels: Custom chrome wires, 15 x 7 (front) 16 x 8 (rear)

Tires: Goodyear Eagle GT 215/60 VR15 (front) 225/60 VR16 (rear)

DIMENSIONS

Length: 149 in.   **Width:** 73.4 in.

Height: 63.3 in.   **Wheelbase:** 103.5 in.

Track: 59.6 in. (front) 56.4 in. (rear)

Weight: 2,470 lbs.

Ford MODEL B ROADSTER

Ever since hot rodders began modifying cars in the late 1940s and early 1950s, the popular choice was the 1932 Model B Ford roadster. This quaint custom combines vintage muscle car performance with 1990s high technology.

"...always turns heads."

"Even though it has been updated, this Roadster still retains a certain period charm. The tuck-and-roll bench seat is spacious yet comfy, and visibility is excellent. Turn the key and the Buick V8 shatters the silence. On the road the engine noise is almost deafening and the small windshield offers little protection. But who cares? No matter where you go, this small Deuce Roadster never fails to turn heads on the sidewalk."

Inside, the Deuce has tuck-and-roll upholstery and aftermarket gauges.

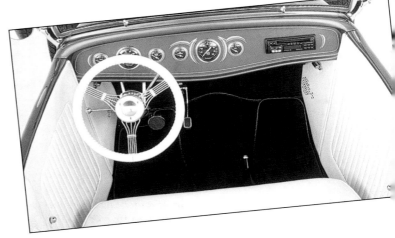

Milestones

1929 Ford launches

its first new car since 1910. Like its predecessor, the Model T, the Model A is available in a variety of body styles, including a convertible Roadster with or without a trunk-mounted rumble seat.

Ford's Model 18 Roadster was very popular when it first appeared and remains so today.

1932 A new series,

the four-cylinder Model B and V8-powered Model 18 replaces the A. The new V8-engined car proves tremendously popular, outselling its sibling by four to one.

The basic engineering of the Model 18 continued into the 1940s with cars like this 1948 Sportsman.

1933 Four-cylinder

models are dropped from the line up and the remaining V8 cars, now known as Model 40s, receive smoother styling with raked-back grills and more flowing fenders. This design is carried over for 1934.

UNDER THE SKIN

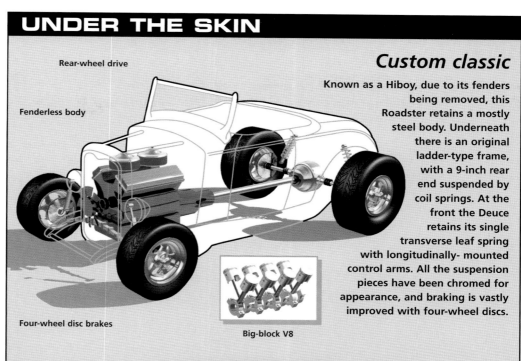

Rear-wheel drive

Fenderless body

Four-wheel disc brakes

Big-block V8

Custom classic

Known as a Hiboy, due to its fenders being removed, this Roadster retains a mostly steel body. Underneath there is an original ladder-type frame, with a 9-inch rear end suspended by coil springs. At the front the Deuce retains its single transverse leaf spring with longitudinally- mounted control arms. All the suspension pieces have been chromed for appearance, and braking is vastly improved with four-wheel discs.

THE POWER PACK

Buick-powered Ford

Most Deuces rely on small-block Chevrolet V8s for power, but the owner of this one chose a different route. Sitting between the frame rails is a 1966 Buick 401-cubic inch V8 taken from a 1966 Wildcat. Named the Nailhead because of its small vertical intake valves, this unit has been reworked with a more aggressive Crane camshaft, an Edelbrock dual-plane manifold and twin 700-cfm four-barrel carburetors. It currently produces 410 bhp.

Two valves per cylinder

Twin four-barrel carburetors

Cast-iron block and cylinder heads

Edelbrock intake manifold

First and best

Early V8 Fords gained immense popularity with hot-rodders in the 1950s, and this trend continues today. The 1932 first-year models are firm favorites and show-quality examples by masters like Boyd Coddington are sold for $70,000 or more.

First-year V8 Roadsters are the most popular with hot-rodders.

Ford **MODEL B ROADSTER**

Named the Deuce because of its model year designation, the 1932 Ford Roadster is as popular today as ever. This one stands out from the crowd with its 1960s custom style and big-block Buick V8 engine.

Buick V8

The owner has chosen a 1960s theme for this car, which includes fitting a 1966 Buick V8 engine.

Opening deck lid

Roadster owners sometimes participate in long-distance hot-rod tours. An opening trunk is practical in that it allows luggage and spare parts to be carried.

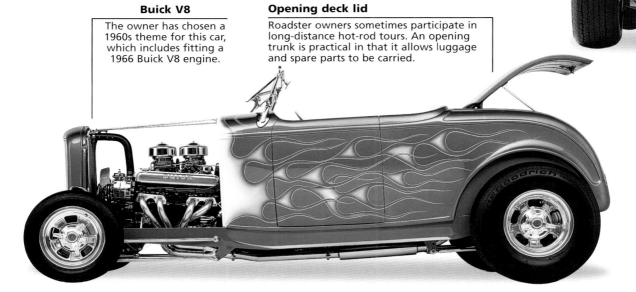

Lowered suspension

Many builders of custom 1932 Fords chose to modify the suspension. This one has been lowered at the front end with cut-down spindles for a raked effect. However, it retains the original-style transverse leaf spring and longitudinally-mounted control arms. At the rear a 9-inch Ford axle is supported by coil springs and shock absorbers.

Stiffening brace

Because there are no fender mountings, a triangular-shaped stiffening brace is attached between the radiator core support and the firewall and helps to reduce chassis flex.

Hinging windshield

Like many cars of the era, the windshield glass can be hinged outward to vent the cabin, although this is not really necessary on this custom Hiboy Roadster.

1932 Ford Roadster

ENGINE

Type: V8

Construction: Cast-iron block and heads

Valve gear: Two valves per cylinder operated by pushrods and rockers

Bore and stroke: 4.2 in. x 3.6 in.

Displacement: 401 c.i.

Compression ratio: 10.25:1

Induction system: Two Holley four-barrel carburetors

Maximum power: 410 bhp at 4,400 rpm

Maximum torque: 445 lb-ft at 2,800 rpm

Top speed: 120 mph

0-60 mph: 5.8 sec.

TRANSMISSION

GM 700R4 four-speed automatic

BODY/CHASSIS

Steel ladder-type frame chassis with separate two-door Roadster body

SPECIAL FEATURES

On this custom Roadster the firewall has been chromed.

At the rear the exhausts exit through the valance.

RUNNING GEAR

Steering: Recirculating ball

Front suspension: Transverse leaf spring with upper and lower control arms and shock absorbers

Rear suspension: Ford 9-in. live rear axle with coil springs and shock absorbers

Brakes: Discs, 9.5-in. dia. (front), 7.5-in. dia. (rear)

Wheels: Chromed Halibrand, 14-in. dia. (front), 16-in. dia. (rear)

Tires: BF Goodrich radials

DIMENSIONS

Length: 132.4 in.   **Width:** 63.9 in.

Height: 51.0 in.   **Wheelbase:** 106.5 in.

Track: 56.2 in. (front), 55.3 in. (rear)

Weight: 2,338 lbs.

Ford MODEL T

One of the true hot-rodding classics, the Model T changed from a form of cheap transportation for everyday people to the outrageous and powerful monsters of a determined group of individuals.

"...California dreamin'."

"The T-bucket Ford hot rod has literally become famous in the songs and legends of Americana. In fact, when rodders are California dreamin', this is the car they see. You're cruisin' the strip on a summer night, staring over all that naked engine roaring in front of you. Jump on the chrome gas pedal and smoke those big rear tires just for fun. It's a car that's happier travelling in a straight line—whether cruising along or embarrassing sportscar drivers at traffic lights. This is what California dreamin' is all about."

The T-bucket's steering column sprouts from the floor and the wheel is almost horizontal, which takes some getting used to.

Milestones

1908 Model T is introduced on October 1—305 cars are built by the end of the year.

1909 Ford introduces its own sporting Model T, the Runabout, with stripped-down bodywork.

The Runabout is a stripped-out Model T roadster.

1915 Production reaches one million and the T has become a common sight on the roads of the world.

The engine in standard Model T only offered 20-bhp.

1927 Production ends after more than 15 million have been built.

1940s & 1950s Hot-rodding craze begins. The Model T is a popular choice because so many are still available.

1960s T-bucket style is created, and the Model T becomes a popular rod to modify once again.

UNDER THE SKIN

Tuned V8 engine

Stripped bodywork

Transverse leaf front suspension

Ford or Chevrolet V8

THE POWER PACK

Different strokes

There are various kinds of hot-rodded Model Ts. The cars built in the 1920s were usually stripped-down roadsters fitted with Model T speed equipment from a vast array of manufacturers. T-buckets have extended chassis with a jacked-up rear-end. All Model T hot rods are fitted with well-located stronger rear axles to deal with the engine's extra power. The chassis is also strengthened to handle the power of the power of a V8 engine.

Eight is great

Although engines vary, almost all of those used are of a V8 configuration. Earlier cars tend to use hopped-up Ford flathead V8s, but in more recent years, the small-block Chevy V8 has proved to be the most popular choice, due mainly to a ready source of second-hand engines and a booming market of tuning parts suppliers. Its simple and strong construction also attracts hot rodders. The car featured on the overleaf has a Corvette, 350-cubic inch small-block V8 modified with a Holley four barrel carburetor and custom headers.

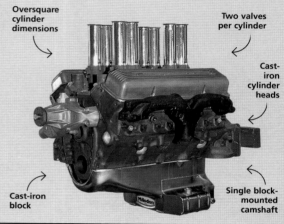

Oversquare cylinder dimensions

Two valves per cylinder

Cast-iron cylinder heads

Single block-mounted camshaft

Cast-iron block

Terrifying T-bucket

The T-bucket is a style of Model T-based hot rod that became popular in the latter half of the sixties. The basic ingredients are minimal bodywork, skinny front and huge rear tires and a powerful American V8 engine (sometimes supercharged) up front. The chassis is strengthened to take the extra power, and lengthened to keep the engine set well back from the front wheels.

The T-bucket was a popular hot rod in the 1960s and 1970s.

Ford MODEL T

The T-bucket is perhaps the best known form of hot-rodded Model T, and is most certainly the most outrageous. It spawned a whole industry making replica Model T parts.

Automatic transmission

This T-bucket is equipped with a GM four-speed automatic transmission and a Hurst shifter.

Disc brakes

The original Model T had weak brakes. With more power, however, a V8-powered T-bucket requires discs brakes.

Wide rear tires

With so much power to transmit to the road, a V8 T-Bucket requires extremely wide tires. They are also installed for visual effect. This car's tires are fitted to Wolfrace Slot Mag wheels, which were a very popular style in the 1970s.

Buttoned-leather interior

Many T-buckets, such as this one, have bench seats, trimmed in buttoned leather, similar to the original Model T.

Skinny front tires

Because the emphasis is on style and straight-line acceleration rather than cornering power, the front tires are very narrow. On this example, motorcycle tires are used at the front.

Jacked-up rear end

Part of the T-Bucket style is to have jacked-up rear suspension, which was popular on many 1960s and 1970s hot rods.

Fold-down windshield

The flat, folding windshield used on the original Model T is retained on the T-bucket It doesn't do much forthe aerodynamics,but is part of this T-bucket's style.

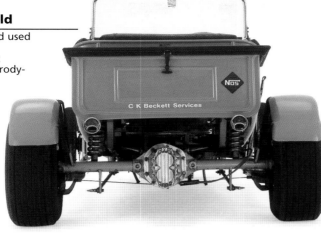

Small-Block Chevy engine

The Small-Block Chevy is a popular engine choice for hot rodders, due to the extensive range of tuning parts available.

Drop-tube front axle

A drop-tube front axle is commonly used on T-Buckets to lower the front end of the car. Chroming is done purely for good looks.

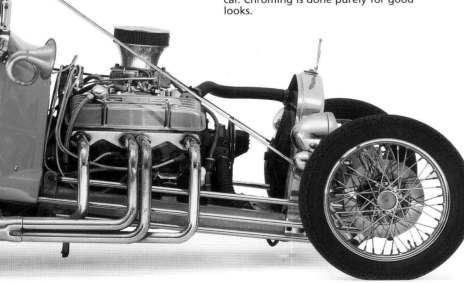

Specifications
1918 Modified Ford Model T

ENGINE

Type: Chevrolet V8
Construction: Cast-iron block and cylinder heads
Valve gear: Two valves per cylinder actuated by a single block-mounted camshaft via pushrods, rocker arms and hydraulic lifters
Bore and stroke: 4 in. x 3.48 in.
Displacement: 350 c.i.
Compression ratio: 10.0:1
Induction system: Holley four-barrel carburetor on an aluminum 'Street Dominator' intake manifold
Maximum power: 250 bhp at 5,000 rpm
Maximum torque: 328 lb-ft at 3,200 rpm
Top speed: 115 mph
0-60 mph: 5.2 sec.

TRANSMISSION

GM four-speed automatic transmission with Hurst shifter

BODY/CHASSIS

Two-seater Model T body on strengthened and lengthened steel chassis

SPECIAL FEATURES

T-bucket retains the original style of front suspension, but the transverse leaf spring is chrome-plated.

Chevrolet small-block V8 engine is topped with a Holley four-barrel carburetor for improved performance.

RUNNING GEAR

Steering: Recirculating ball
Front suspension: Solid axle, transverse leaf spring with telescopic shocks
Rear suspension: Live axle with trailing arms, coil springs and telescopic shocks
Brakes: Four-wheel discs
Wheels: Spoked steel (front) Wolfrace Slot Mag Alloy (rear)
Tires: 145/70-16 (front), 275/60-ZR15 (rear)

DIMENSIONS

Length: 11.7 in.   **Width:** 68.8 in.
Height: 49.7 in.   **Wheelbase:** 90 in.
Track: 55.7 in. (front), 56.2 in. (rear)
Weight: 2,198 lbs.

Ford MUSTANG

Following its 1964 launch, the Mustang was a massive hit. Creating a place in the pony car market, its sales continued to increase. A modification of a 1966 car was the next step for this almost perfect package.

"...no ordinary Mustang."

"Do not be fooled by its looks; this is no ordinary Mustang. Underneath there have been a multitude of changes. The supercharged engine delivers considerable power, and the modified chassis gives more stability and poise than the original. Great attention has been paid to the interior, which blends well with the orange exterior. You would be hard-pressed to find a better example of a 1966 Mustang."

The carpet of this car is taken from Mercedes and it certainly looks elegant.

Milestones

1961 Inspirational
Ford President Lee Iacocca decides that the company should produce a sporty-looking car. Prototypes are built using a German four-cylinder engine.

1966 Mustangs came as convertibles as well as hardtops.

1964 Six months
ahead of the 1965 calendar year, Ford releases the Mustang. It is an instant hit, sparking a host of imitators from other manufacturers as the pony car war heats up.

The Mustang's first major design changes were introduced on the 1967 model, a bigger car.

1974 After a series
of styling changes, the original Mustang is replaced by the Mustang II. Initially a strong seller, it falls victim to the impending oil crisis and becomes a bloated, underpowered version of its previous self. Sales suffer as a result.

UNDER THE SKIN

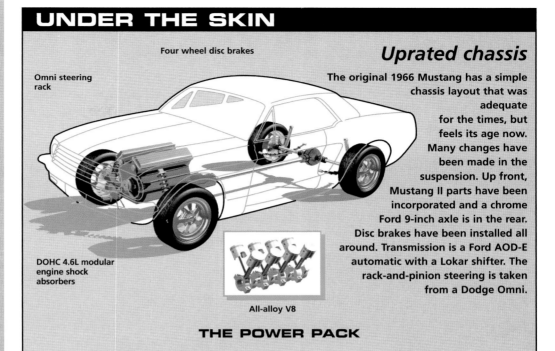

Four wheel disc brakes

Omni steering rack

DOHC 4.6L modular engine shock absorbers

All-alloy V8

Uprated chassis

The original 1966 Mustang has a simple chassis layout that was adequate for the times, but feels its age now. Many changes have been made in the suspension. Up front, Mustang II parts have been incorporated and a chrome Ford 9-inch axle is in the rear. Disc brakes have been installed all around. Transmission is a Ford AOD-E automatic with a Lokar shifter. The rack-and-pinion steering is taken from a Dodge Omni.

THE POWER PACK

4.6 Liter "modular" V8

In 1966, the Mustang was available with a 200-c.i. inline six or a 289-c.i V8, in either 200 bhp or 225/271 bhp state of tune. The venerable cast-iron motor was considered too heavy for this Mustang and has been replaced by a 32-valve, 4.6 liter modular Ford V8 unit with all-alloy construction. From its relatively small displacement, 281 c.i., it produces 392 bhp with the aid of a Kenne Bell twin-screw whipplecharger running at 6 pounds of boost. This is in combination with a multipoint electronic fuel-injection system and a modern engine layout of four valves per cylinder operated by four chain-driven overhead camshafts.

Dynamite

For some people, the pre-1967 Mustangs are the best of the breed. The lines are uncluttered and classic. When mated with a stiff chassis and powerful engine, excellence is created—exactly what this 1966 example is.

Tasteful modifications have not betrayed the Mustang's good looks.

Ford MUSTANG

If you like the looks but not the performance, what can you do? Build your ideal car, of course. With nearly 400 bhp and a chassis that can handle the power, this Mustang would be your dream car.

Tangerine dream

Completing the modified look is the tangerine pearl custom paint scheme. The side scallops are finished in a blend of gold pearl and candy root beer.

Supercharged engine

To get phenomenal performance from the Mustang, a 32-valve, all-alloy 4.6 liter "modular" Ford V8 engine, from a late-model Mustang Cobra, has been fitted. The power has been upped to 392 bhp by the addition of a Kenne Bell supercharger running at 6 pounds of boost.

Billet grill

A lot of attention has been paid to the look of this car. This is illustrated by the six-bar chrome front grill and the five-bar rear fascia, which incorporates 900 LEDs.

Four-wheel disc brakes

To balance the enhanced performance, disc brakes have been installed. At the front these are 11 inches in diameter with 9-inch ones at the rear.

Custom interior

As much work has gone into customizing the interior as modifying the mechanicals of this car. There are two shades of leather upholstery, cream and biscuit. There is also a wool carpet from a Mercedes, as well as modified 1965 T-Bird front seats.

Upgraded suspension

As with many modified first-generation Mustangs, this car uses the coil-sprung front suspension from the Mustang II. A chrome 9-inch rear axle combines with a Global West stage III suspension system out back.

Specifications

1966 Ford Mustang

ENGINE

Type: V8

Construction: Alloy block and heads

Valve gear: Four valves per cylinder operated by four chain-driven overhead cams.

Bore and stroke: 3.61 in. x 3.60 in.

Displacement: 281 c.i.

Compression ratio: 9.8:1

Induction system: Multipoint fuel injection with Kenne Bell twin-screw whipple supercharger

Maximum power: 392 bhp at 5,800 rpm

Maximum torque: 405 lb-ft at 4,500 rpm

Top speed: 141 mph

0-60 mph: 4.3 sec.

TRANSMISSION

Three-speed automatic

BODY/CHASSIS

Steel chassis with steel body

SPECIAL FEATURES

Even the trunk has been upholstered in matching fabrics.

Budnick alloy wheels are a fine addition to the car.

RUNNING GEAR

Steering: Rack-and-pinion

Front suspension: A-arms with coil springs and telescopic shock absorbers

Rear suspension: Live rear axle with leaf springs and telescopic shock absorbers

Brakes: Discs, 11-in. dia. (front), 9-in. dia. (rear)

Wheels: Alloy, 17 x 7 in. (front); 17 x 8 in. (rear)

Tires: Toyo 215/45ZR17 (front), 245/45ZR17 (rear)

DIMENSIONS

Length: 176.0 in. **Width:** 71.0 in.

Height: 50.3 in. **Wheelbase:** 108.0 in.

Track: 58.6 in. (front and rear)

Weight: 2,358 lbs.

Ford **MUSTANG GT**

Fox-bodied Mustangs rekindled America's love affair with performance cars. An easy-to-tweak 5.0-liter V8 is just one reason why these cars are so popular. The owner of this particular car went wild bolting on many aftermarket body panels.

"...spaceship-like exterior"

"Similar to many of its rivals, the driver sits fairly low in the Mustang. The gauges are easy to read and an aftermarket monster tachometer keeps the driver totally informed. The reworked 5.0-liter V8 gives a loud roar when the accelerator pedal hits the floor and the tach needle hits 4,000 rpm. Unlike older Mustangs, this one handles like it's on rails. Its spaceship-like exterior has been modified and the only remaining factory panel is the roof, giving it a one-of-a-kind look."

A set of auxiliary gauges replaces the center air vents and everything is color-coded.

Milestones

1979 A new Mustang, with sharp-edged styling, makes its debut.

1982 After several years of pseudo-performance cars, Ford offers the genuine article in the shape of a new Mustang GT. Producing 157 bhp from a 302-cubic inch V8 and with sports suspension, it is fun to drive.

By 1984, the Mustang GT had a four-barrel carburetor and produced 175 bhp.

1987 A heavily-facelifted Mustang goes on sale. The V8 is available in both GT and LX models.

The pinnacle of 'Fox' Mustang development was the 1993 SVT Cobra.

1993 This year sees the end of 'Fox'-platform Mustangs, and a special Cobra is released. It looks similar to the GT, but has larger wheels and tires, slightly different styling and an engine tweaked to 240 bhp.

UNDER THE SKIN

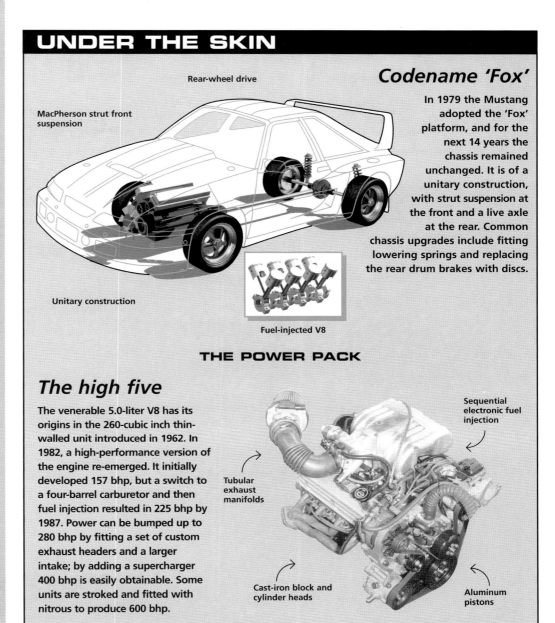

Rear-wheel drive

MacPherson strut front suspension

Unitary construction

Fuel-injected V8

Codename 'Fox'

In 1979 the Mustang adopted the 'Fox' platform, and for the next 14 years the chassis remained unchanged. It is of a unitary construction, with strut suspension at the front and a live axle at the rear. Common chassis upgrades include fitting lowering springs and replacing the rear drum brakes with discs.

THE POWER PACK

The high five

The venerable 5.0-liter V8 has its origins in the 260-cubic inch thin-walled unit introduced in 1962. In 1982, a high-performance version of the engine re-emerged. It initially developed 157 bhp, but a switch to a four-barrel carburetor and then fuel injection resulted in 225 bhp by 1987. Power can be bumped up to 280 bhp by fitting a set of custom exhaust headers and a larger intake; by adding a supercharger 400 bhp is easily obtainable. Some units are stroked and fitted with nitrous to produce 600 bhp.

Sequential electronic fuel injection

Tubular exhaust manifolds

Cast-iron block and cylinder heads

Aluminum pistons

Street or track

'Fox'-platform Mustangs are an ideal base for one-off street machines. Most are turned into drag-style rides, but these cars also make fantastic street freaks as well. There is often no limit to what can be achieved, given the money and imagination.

Thanks to the aftermarket, modifications to 1980s Mustangs are limitless.

Ford **MUSTANG GT**

More than a million 'Fox' Mustangs were built between 1979 and 1993 and, today, they are perhaps America's favorite late-model street machines. In addition, an entire aftermarket industry is devoted to these cars.

V8 engine

The 5.0-liter V8 has been bored .030 over, fortified with ceramic-coated headers, a K&N filter, an ACUFAB Billet throttle body and a high-lift camshaft. This results in an increase of power from 225 to 370 bhp.

Opening hatch

An opening decklid offers a useful amount of space, but body stiffness suffers as a result.

Steeper gearing

The Mustang 5.0-liter came with 2.73 or 3.08 rear gears. For better acceleration, the rear end has been fitted with 3.55 cogs.

Outlandish rear wing

Subtle is not a word used to describe this Mustang. It is modified with full MPH body extensions, including a large IMSA-type rear wing.

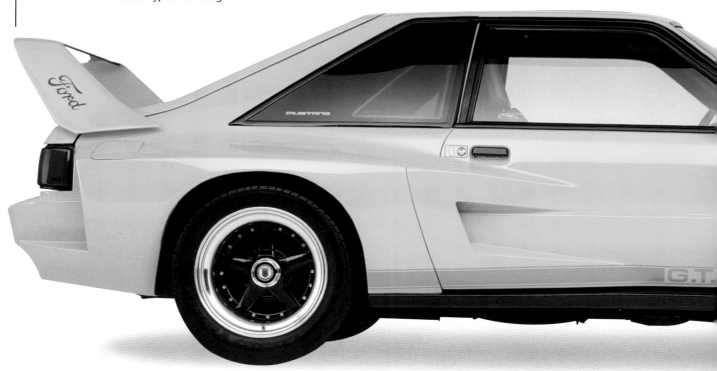

Road racing suspension

Corner carving and head turning is what this Mustang GT was built to do. To help it zig, it has been lowered with a Saleen Racecraft suspension.

Cowl induction hood

A popular aftermarket addition is a fiberglass cowl induction hood. This draws high-pressure air from the base of the windshield, forcing it through the intake and thus increasing power.

Specifications
1987 Ford Mustang GT

ENGINE
Type: V8

Construction: Cast-iron block and heads

Valve gear: Two valves per cylinder operated by pushrods and rockers

Bore and stroke: 4.0 in. x 3.0 in.

Displacement: 306 c.i.

Compression ratio: 10.0:1

Induction system: Sequential electronic fuel injection

Maximum power: 370 bhp at 4,800 rpm

Maximum torque: 300 lb-ft at 3,000 rpm

Top speed: 150 mph

0-60 mph: 5.2 sec.

TRANSMISSION
Borg-Warner 'World Class' T-5 five-speed manual

BODY/CHASSIS
Unitary monocoque with steel and fiberglass three-door hatchback body

SPECIAL FEATURES

A very distinctive feature of this car is its high rear wing.

Ford's 5.0-liter V8 is an easy engine to tune for more power.

RUNNING GEAR
Steering: Recirculating ball

Front suspension: MacPherson struts with coil springs and telescopic shock absorbers

Rear suspension: Live axle with coil springs and quad telescopic shock absorbers

Brakes: Vented discs (front), discs (rear)

Wheels: HRE alloy, 10 x 17 in. (front), 13 x 17 in. (rear)

Tires: 17-in. dia

DIMENSIONS
Length: 178.0 in.   **Width:** 78.2 in.

Height: 48.3 in.   **Wheelbase:** 100.4 in.

Track: 63.0 in. (front), 64.0 in. (rear)

Weight: 3,560 lbs.

Ford ROADSTER

If any car typifies the classic hot rod, it has to be the 1932 Ford Hi-boy Roadster. In the late 1940s and early 1950s, young men back from World War II wanted fast cars for low dollars. Stripping a Ford Roadster down to its bare bones and fitting a hot V8 was one of the most popular methods.

"...a nostalgic road rocket."

"If you're shy, then this car isn't for you. This Hi-boy, nostalgic, road rocket is a style icon today and can't help turning heads. The short stub exhaust pipes don't help either—the loud V8 rumble is deafening at higher engine speeds. It's only when the road clears that you realize that this car goes as as great as it looks. It doesn't weigh much and the engine puts out an unstressed 250 bhp, so acceleration is incredible. It takes a brave man to drive it at over 100 mph, though."

Stewart Warner, white-faced gauges give this hot rod a classic look.

Milestones

1931 With sales dropping due to the Depression, Chevrolet edges ahead of Ford in model-year sales figures.

Replacing the Model A for 1932 was the new four-cylinder Model B and V8 Model 18.

1932 In response, Ford improves its cars.

The old, squared-off exposed radiator is replaced by a new smoother radiator cowl. This year also sees the launch of the famous Flathead V8. The four-cylinder Model B range is sold alongside the V8 Model 18s.

1932 Fords are still popular today, but fashions have indeed changed.

1933 The Ford lineup gets new graceful, low-slung styling.

UNDER THE SKIN

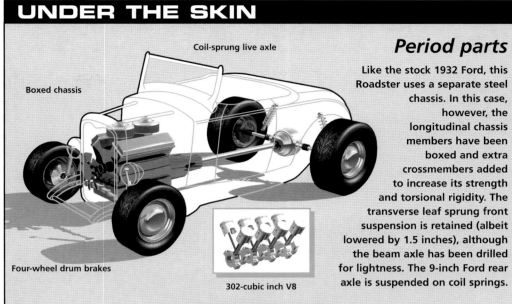

Coil-sprung live axle

Boxed chassis

Four-wheel drum brakes

302-cubic inch V8

Period parts

Like the stock 1932 Ford, this Roadster uses a separate steel chassis. In this case, however, the longitudinal chassis members have been boxed and extra crossmembers added to increase its strength and torsional rigidity. The transverse leaf sprung front suspension is retained (albeit lowered by 1.5 inches), although the beam axle has been drilled for lightness. The 9-inch Ford rear axle is suspended on coil springs.

THE POWER PACK

Windsor power

Although the most authentic Hi-boys tend to use Ford Flatheads, many others use more modern V8s. This particular car uses a 1969 Ford 302-cubic inch Windsor V8. It has been mildly tuned with a high-lift Crower camshaft, free-flowing tubular-steel headers, a high-rise Offenhauser intake manifold and a 600-cfm Holley four-barrel carburetor. All this takes the maximum power to a reliable 250 bhp at 4,500 rpm and 275 lb-ft of torque at 3,000 rpm.

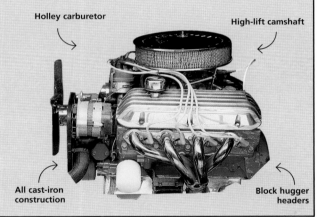

Holley carburetor

High-lift camshaft

All cast-iron construction

Block hugger headers

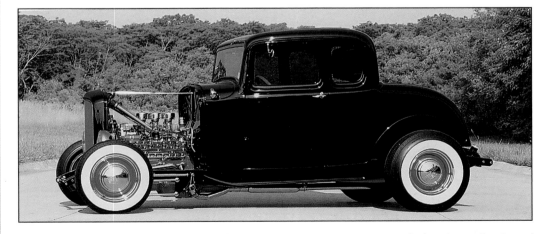

Top rods

Although there are many different styles of hot rod based on the 1932 Ford, these original-style Hi-boys are real classics and even considered so by many enthusiasts of stock classic and vintage cars. They are part of America's post-war heritage, along with drive-in movies and rock and roll music.

Black paint and red steel wheels are classic 1950s hot rod touches.

Ford **ROADSTER**

To many, the first image that comes to mind when you say 'hot rod' would probably be something like this classic 1950s-style Hi-boy based on a 1932 Ford Roadster. Its simplicity of concept—less weight, more power—makes it a great and stylish custom.

Ford V8

The 1932 Ford Model 18 came with the then-new Flathead V8 engine. This car has a Ford 302-cubic inch Windsor V8. Mild tuning ensures reliability while still producing 250 bhp.

Drum brakes

Like the original car, this Hi-boy has four-wheel drum brakes. The front drums have been taken from a 1949 Buick and are finned to improve cooling and reduce brake fade.

Rumble seat

There were two styles of the 1932 Roadster. Externally they looked identical, but one version, such as this model, had a rumble seat in the trunk to carry extra passengers.

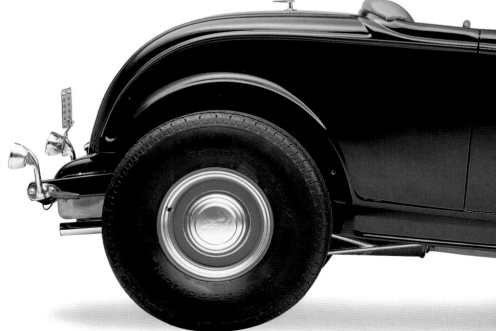

Fenderless styling

The first thing an early hot-rodder would do with his Ford would be to remove the floor boards and fenders. This cut weight and gave easier access to the mechanicals. The lack of fenders is the most important part of the classic Hi-boy look but can cause problems on wet roads—not only do you get wet with the spray from the front tires, but any cars following behind will be blinded by the huge fountains of spray from the massive rear tires.

Beam axle

The 1932 Ford used a beam axle and transverse leaf spring for the front suspension. This car has had the front end lowered by 1.5 inches for the classic nose-down stance and the axle has been drilled to reduce weight.

Steel wheels

With alloy wheels not yet available, the only options were pressed-steel or wire-spoked wheels. These were often painted in bright contrasting colors to liven them up.

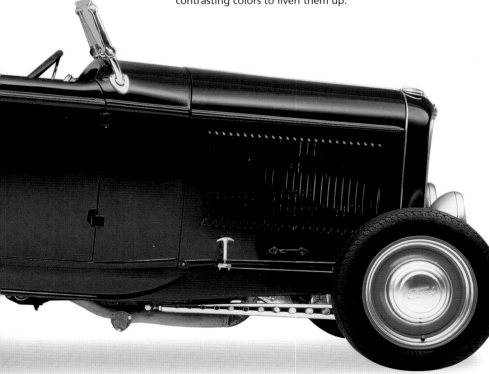

Specifications

1932 Ford Hi-Boy Roadster

ENGINE

Type: V8

Construction: Cast-iron block and heads

Valve gear: Two valves per cylinder operated by a single camshaft with pushrods and rockers

Bore and stroke: 4.00 in. x 3.00 in.

Displacement: 302 c.i.

Compression ratio: 9.0:1

Induction system: Holley 600-cfm four-barrel carburetor

Maximum power: 250 bhp at 4,500 rpm

Maximum torque: 275 lb-ft at 3,000 rpm

Top speed: 120 mph

0-60 mph: 6.0 sec.

TRANSMISSION

Three-speed manual

BODY/CHASSIS

Steel chassis and steel and fiberglass body

SPECIAL FEATURES

The Roadster body style comes complete with a folding windshield.

Big-finned 1949 Buick front drums gives much improved braking.

RUNNING GEAR

Steering: Recirculating ball

Front suspension: Beam axle with transverse leaf springs, parallel control arms and telescopic shock absorbers

Rear suspension: Live axle with coil springs and telescopic shock absorbers

Brakes: Drums (front and rear)

Wheels: Steel, 15-in. dia. (front and rear)

Tires: 145 SR15 (front), 33 x 12.50 R15 (rear)

DIMENSIONS

Length: 132.5 in.   **Width:** 63.9 in.

Height: 52.0 in.   **Wheelbase:** 106.5 in.

Track: 56.2 in. (front), 56.2 in. (rear)

Weight: 2,250 lbs.

Ford **THUNDERBIRD**

The 1955 Thunderbird was the first of a legendary line of Fords and was designed to compete with Chevrolet's Corvette. The Thunderbird was always more of a 'personal' car than an outright sports car. This example has been personalized much further with a 630-bhp supercharged V8.

"...seamless wall of torque."

"It's easy to feel at home once you are settled behind the wheel of this Thunderbird. The interior is a fantastic mix of classic 1950s feel with a slight techno edge. The monster V8 gives effortless performance, while the supercharger lends the engine a seamless wall of torque. The computer-designed suspension gives the T-bird handling that the original could never have dreamed of, and the four-wheel disc brake system stops the car with ease."

This Thunderbird has a subtle modern edge to its classic 1950s interior.

Milestones

1955 Two years after Chevrolet

launched the Corvette, Ford releases the V8-engined Thunderbird to rival it. More than 16,000 are sold in its first year, massively outselling the Corvette.

A 1971 Boss 351 Mustang gave up its Cleveland V8 for this modified 1955 T-bird.

1956 The T-bird gets an optional

312-cubic inch engine, an exterior-mount spare, softer suspension and an optional 'Porthole' hardtop.

The T-bird debuted as a 1955 model with an optional 292-cubic inch V8.

1957 Ford launches the last two-seater T-bird.

A facelift added a more prominent grill and a longer deck. There is also more power and even a limited run of supercharged cars. The T-bird becomes a less sporty four-seater the following year.

UNDER THE SKIN

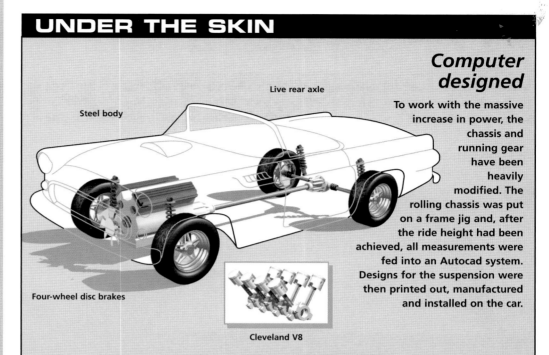

Steel body

Live rear axle

Four-wheel disc brakes

Cleveland V8

Computer designed

To work with the massive increase in power, the chassis and running gear have been heavily modified. The rolling chassis was put on a frame jig and, after the ride height had been achieved, all measurements were fed into an Autocad system. Designs for the suspension were then printed out, manufactured and installed on the car.

THE POWER PACK

Blown Boss

Gone is the original 292-cubic inch Mercury V8, replaced by a seriously-modified 351 Cleveland V8. It has been overbored to give a new displacement of 361 cubic inches and has a billet crankshaft and connecting rods. Forged pistons and early-style Yates NASCAR aluminum heads give an 8.2:1 compression ratio. There is also a NASCAR aluminum radiator to keep the engine operating at a reasonable temperature. The Custom-designed fuel injection system and Vortech supercharger, running 6 lbs. of boost, help this radical motor to pump out 630 bhp at 6,800 rpm and 550 lb-ft of torque at 4,900 rpm.

Blown 'Bird

Ford designers got the shape of the original Thunderbird just right, so there was no need to change it. This car retains its original styling but has the added bonus of earth-shattering performance and modern standards of handling and braking.

The owner of this model has left the bodywork largely untouched.

Ford **THUNDERBIRD**

Two of Ford's most legendary cars of all time are the Mustang and the Thunderbird. This may be a 1955 two-seat T-bird, but under the hood beats the heart of a Mustang, in this case a blown Boss 351 Cleveland.

Supercharged V8

Under the hood, there is a 351 Cleveland unit instead of the original 292-cubic inch mill. A Vortech supercharger, aluminum NASCAR heads and a custom fuel injection system help take the power output to a heady 630 bhp.

Powerful brakes

The Thunderbird's original drum brake setup would be nearly useless on this road rocket. This car is fitted with a twin master cylinder brake system with 11-inch Camaro front discs and Lincoln rear discs.

Bulletproof rear end

The ubiquitous 9-inch Ford rear axle sits under this car, with 4.56:1 gears and a limited-slip differ-ential for maximum traction off the line.

Custom interior

The interior retains the factory styling but is brought up to date with digital instruments. The front seat has been specially fitted for the driver to give a perfect and comfortable driving position.

Rack-and-pinion steering

The old recirculating ball steering has been replaced with Mustang II spindles and a power-assisted rack-and-pinion steering system.

Near-stock body

This car retains its original steel body. The only modifications are the shaved trunk and doors. It is finished in striking Black Plum paint.

Specifications

1955 Ford Thunderbird

ENGINE

Type: V8

Construction: Cast-iron block and aluminum heads

Valve gear: Two valves per cylinder operated by a single camshaft with pushrods and hydraulic lifters

Bore and stroke: 4.06 in. x 3.50 in.

Displacement: 361 c.i.

Compression ratio: 8.2:1

Induction system: Custom fuel injection and Vortech supercharger

Maximum power: 630 bhp at 6,800 rpm

Maximum torque: 550 lb-ft at 4,900 rpm

Top speed: 165 mph

0-60 mph: 3.6 sec.

TRANSMISSION

Ford A40D automatic transmission

BODY/CHASSIS

Steel chassis and steel two-seater body

SPECIAL FEATURES

Digital gauges in the original housings are a neat touch.

A custom-built fuel injection system helps to produce 630 bhp.

RUNNING GEAR

Steering: Rack-and-pinion

Front suspension: Tubular A-arms with coil springs and telescopic shock absorbers

Rear suspension: Tubular A-arms with coil springs and telescopic shock absorbers

Brakes: Discs (front and rear)

Wheels: Weld Racing alloy, 15-in. dia.

Tires: Winston Radials

DIMENSIONS

Length: 175.3 in. **Width:** 70.3 in.

Height: 49.2 in. **Wheelbase:** 102.0 in.

Track: 57.8 in. (front), 55.86 in. (rear)

Weight: 2,980 lbs.

Ford WOODY

A custom station wagon with real wood paneling was part of Ford's 1950 model line. Today these wagons, often called Woodys, are a favorite with car customizers young and old.

"...Built for straight-line speed."

"Equipped with a supercharged small-block Chevy V8, this Woody is quick off the line and hauls itself up to 60 mph in less than six seconds. Big rear tires provide excellent grip and enable rapid dragster-style launches from the lights. Although built for straight-line speed, the car retains relatively large front tires to provide some concession toward cornering grip and large disc brakes to make deceleration safer and quicker than the original drums."

This pro-street car has a custom interior with an electrically-adjustable front bench seat.

Milestones

1949 An all new

Ford with independent front suspension makes its debut. Topping the line is the $2,000 Custom Wagon with real wood inserts. Two engines are available, a straight-six and the venerable 'Flathead V8.'

The 1950 Mercury was similar to the Ford, but more luxurious.

1950 The Custom

wagon is renamed Country Squire and all models receive a mild facelift with a revised grill. Handling and build quality are vastly improved over the 1949 car.

Henry Ford's original V8 engine was still powering Fords in 1950.

1951 Returning for

its final season, the wood-framed station wagon is now available with a three-speed Ford-O-Matic transmission. Ford debuts its all steel bodied station wagons for 1952.

UNDER THE SKIN

Exclusively Ford

The original Ford chassis has been retained, but modified with a Mustang front suspension consisting of unequal length wishbones, coil springs and telescopic shocks. At the rear is a narrowed Ford rear axle with 4.11 gears. Ladder bars prevent wheel hop under hard acceleration and four-wheel disc brakes taken from a Lincoln enable safe stopping.

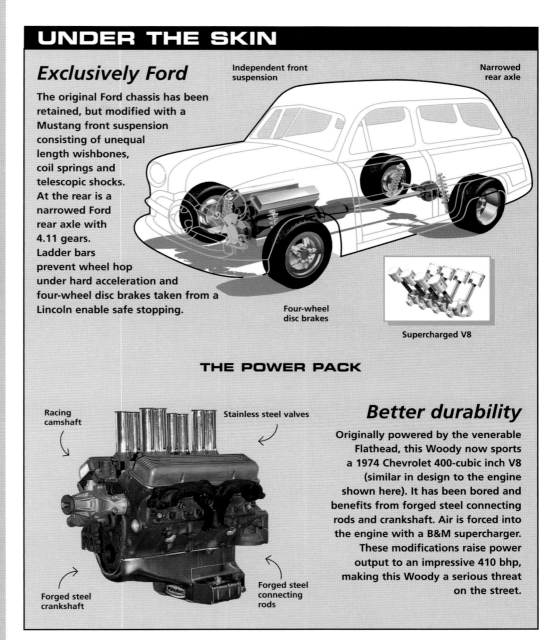

Independent front suspension

Narrowed rear axle

Four-wheel disc brakes

Supercharged V8

THE POWER PACK

Racing camshaft

Stainless steel valves

Forged steel crankshaft

Forged steel connecting rods

Better durability

Originally powered by the venerable Flathead, this Woody now sports a 1974 Chevrolet 400-cubic inch V8 (similar in design to the engine shown here). It has been bored and benefits from forged steel connecting rods and crankshaft. Air is forced into the engine with a B&M supercharger. These modifications raise power output to an impressive 410 bhp, making this Woody a serious threat on the street.

1950 Woody

A Country Squire wagon was the most expensive Ford you could buy in 1950 and was only available in two-door form. Today, along with the Chevrolet Nomad, they rank as one of the most popular American station wagons of all time.

Even today the 1950 Woodys have popular, yet unusual, appeal.

Ford WOODY

The 1950s Fords were very popular custom cars in the 1960s. This 1950 Woody has been updated with modern running gear while retaining a classic yet custom look.

Modified hood

In order to accommodate the large supercharger mounted on top of the engine the hood has been modified so the enormous air scoop can protrude through it.

Air conditioning

Although the back seat has been removed, the owner still wants some comfort, so a custom air conditioning system is fitted.

Tinted windows

Woodys are a fashion statement in California and this one has tinted windows to enhance its street credibility.

Predominantly steel

Most of the body is built from steel, only the doors, tailgate and quarter panels are fabricated from real wood.

Chevrolet V8 engine

In its day, the Ford Flathead V8 was the powerplant of choice for hot rodding. Today its place has been taken by the ubiquitous small-block Chevy V8. This one features dual four-barrel carburetors and a supercharger to help it achieve its 410 bhp at 5,100 rpm.

Subtle modification

Although the body remains fairly standard, the tailgate features taillights taken from a 1946 Ford.

Specifications
1950 Ford Woody

ENGINE

Type: V8

Construction: Cast-iron block and heads

Valve gear: Two valves per cylinder operated by pushrods and rockers

Bore/stroke: 4.18 in. x 3.75 in.

Displacement: 406 c.i.

Compression ratio: 8.0:1

Induction system: Two four-barrel Holley 600 cfm carburetors

Maximum power: 410 bhp at 5,100 rpm

Maximum torque: 450 lb-ft at 3,100 rpm

Top speed: 147 mph

0-60 mph: 4.7 sec.

TRANSMISSION

GM 700R4 four-speed automatic with 2,500 stall torque converter and overdrive lockout

BODY/CHASSIS

Separate chassis with steel and wood two-door body

SPECIAL FEATURES

Supercharger assembly requires a cutout in the hood for clearance and for feeding air to the Chevy V8.

The center grill spinner bears an uncanny resemblance to that used on the contemporary Studebaker Champion.

RUNNING GEAR

Steering: Recirculating ball

Front suspension: Unequal length wishbones, coil springs and telescopic shocks

Rear suspension: Narrowed live axle with ladder bars and coil springs and telescopic shocks

Brakes: Four-wheel discs

Wheels: American Racing Torque Thrust D 7 x 15 (front) 10 x 15 (rear)

Tires: BF Goodrich radials (front) Mickey Thompson Prostreets (rear)

DIMENSIONS

Length: 174 in.   **Width:** 73.3 in.

Height: 56.7 in.   **Wheelbase:** 114 in.

Track: 56.5 in. (front) 50.2 in. (rear)

Weight: 3,402 lbs.

Hudson **SUPER SIX**

In 1948, Hudson introduced its 'step-down' range. Smooth and sleek, the Super Six has a low center of gravity and makes an excellent, though unusual, starting point for a lead sled. Custom body work and a modern fuel injected engine makes a very radically modified Hudson hot rod.

"...attention wherever it goes."

"Classic style meets 1990s technology—that's the best description of the interior of this Hudson. The custom upholstery contrasts with the small windows and the classic steering wheel. With a late-model LT1® V8 engine and automatic transmission, performance is good. But this car feels most at home cruising the strip and attracting attention wherever it goes."

No expense has been spared on this incredible customized Hudson, including radical changes to the interior.

Milestones

1948 After fielding

warmed-over 1942 models for the past two years, Hudson introduces its radical 'step-down'. An all-new straight-six engine makes these Hudsons some of the fastest cars on sale in America.

1951 Hudson introduces

the powerful Hornet with an enlarged straight-six engine.

From any angle the Hudson 'step-down' looks sleek.

1952 Although the

Hornet proves to be an outstanding success in NASCAR, sales begin to slump due to lack of change. Hudson cannot afford tooling for a new body.

Hudson's Hornet was a successful NASCAR competitor.

1954 The 'step-down' returns for its last

year. Styling is very dated, despite an attractive facelift.

UNDER THE SKIN

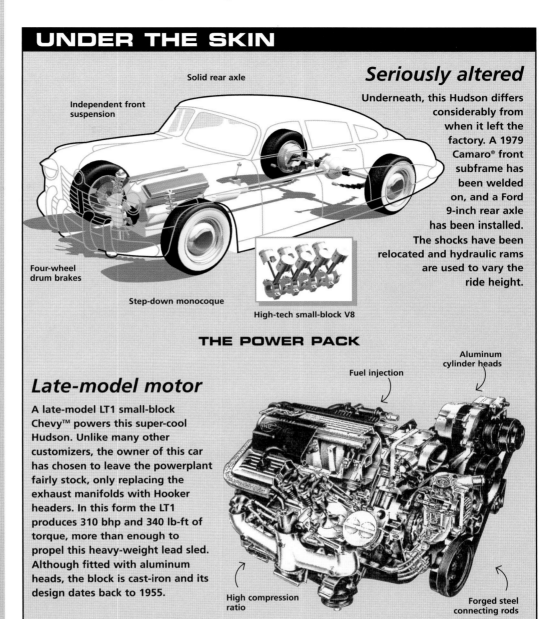

Solid rear axle

Independent front suspension

Four-wheel drum brakes

Step-down monocoque

High-tech small-block V8

Seriously altered

Underneath, this Hudson differs considerably from when it left the factory. A 1979 Camaro® front subframe has been welded on, and a Ford 9-inch rear axle has been installed. The shocks have been relocated and hydraulic rams are used to vary the ride height.

THE POWER PACK

Late-model motor

A late-model LT1 small-block Chevy™ powers this super-cool Hudson. Unlike many other customizers, the owner of this car has chosen to leave the powerplant fairly stock, only replacing the exhaust manifolds with Hooker headers. In this form the LT1 produces 310 bhp and 340 lb-ft of torque, more than enough to propel this heavy-weight lead sled. Although fitted with aluminum heads, the block is cast-iron and its design dates back to 1955.

Fuel injection

Aluminum cylinder heads

High compression ratio

Forged steel connecting rods

Sleek shape

Although radical when it first appeared in 1948, the Hudson 'step-down' was a monocoque which made it difficult to alter. This meant that sales soon began to fall, despite the advent of the sporty Hornet. True Hudsons were history after 1954.

Even stock Hudson Sixes look low and perform well.

Hudson **SUPER SIX**

No expense was spared during the creation of this one-of-a-kind Hudson Super Six. The list of modifications is almost endless, and the result is a striking and unique car.

Custom hinges
Even the trunk-lid hinges have been altered, with the deck lid hinging to the right on opening.

Sun visor
Despite the radical contemporary modifications, this Hudson is fitted with a period 1940s sun visor. On this car it is perfectly blended into the roof line.

Special wheels
Full dish aluminum wheels, like those used on Bonneville flats racers, are fitted and stand out against the dark paintwork.

Shaved doors
The doors have been 'shaved' of their handles and locks. Thanks to modern electronics, this lead sled uses a device that electronically activcates latches hidden inside the doors to allow easy entry.

Fastback shape
Fastbacks were in vogue in the late 1940s. At the time of its introduction the 'step-down' Hudson had one of the sleekest shapes around. A low center of gravity ensures good handling.

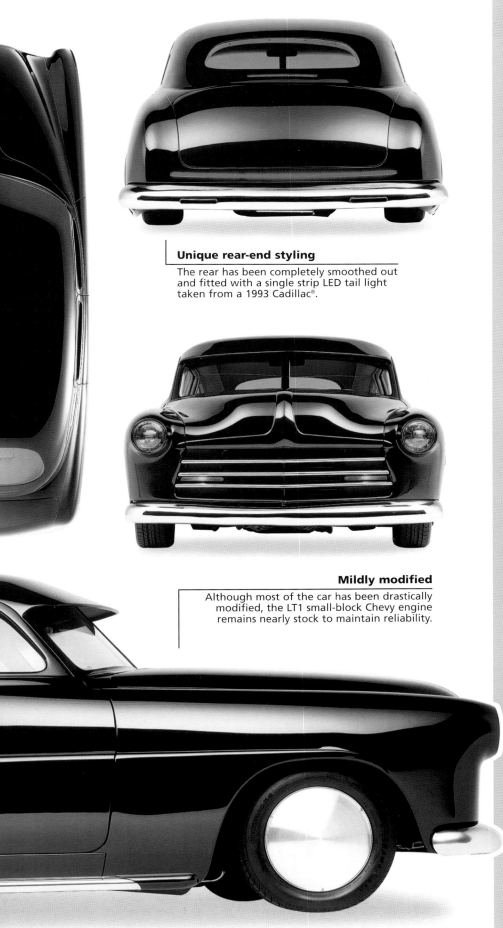

Unique rear-end styling

The rear has been completely smoothed out
and fitted with a single strip LED tail light
taken from a 1993 Cadillac®.

Mildly modified

Although most of the car has been drastically
modified, the LT1 small-block Chevy engine
remains nearly stock to maintain reliability.

Specifications

1949 Hudson Super Six

ENGINE

Type: V8

Construction: Cast-iron block with
aluminum heads

Valve gear: Two valves per cylinder
operated by pushrods and rockers

Bore and stroke: 4 in. x 3.48 in.

Displacement: 350 c.i.

Compression ratio: 10.5:1

Induction system: Multiport electronic
fuel injection

Maximum power: 310 bhp at 5,000 rpm

Maximum torque: 340 lb-ft at 2,400 rpm

Top speed: 124 mph

0-60 mph: 9.0 sec.

TRANSMISSION

GM 700R4 four-speed automatic

BODY/CHASSIS

Dropped floorpan monocoque

SPECIAL FEATURES

**Flip-out door
mirrors are a
unique feature
on this
customized
lead sled.**

**Even the valve covers have been
custom-made and include Hudson script.**

RUNNING GEAR

Steering: Recirculating ball

Front suspension: Unequal length
wishbones with hydraulic rams and
telescopic shocks

Rear suspension: Live axle with
hydraulic rams, Watt linkage, and
telescopic shocks

Brakes: Servo-assisted drums

Wheels: Custom alloy, 15-in. dia.

Tires: Firestone Firehawk F670-15.

DIMENSIONS

Length: 195.6 in. **Width:** 73.4 in.

Height: 54 in. **Wheelbase:** 124 in.

Track: 60.4 in. (front), 57.6 in. (rear)

Weight: 3,554 lbs.

Kaiser MANHATTAN

A second-generation Kaiser made its debut in 1951. One of the most stylish and best-handling cars of its day, it makes a very distinctive and unusual basis for a pro street ride.

"...maximum thrills."

"A large windshield provides excellent outward visibility, and although the multiple shades of purple take some getting used to, the interior is practical and functional. A highly-modified blown small-block engine provides the power and, with the big tires and roll cage, off the line acceleration is excellent. The shifts from the automatic transmission are precise and in less than 10 seconds you have covered the ¼-mile. This car really does deliver maximum thrills."

Multiple shades of purple greet the driver while custom bucket seats offer good support.

Milestones

1947 Industrialist Henry J. Kaiser and

business partner Joseph Frazer build their first car, which wears both Frazer and Kaiser badging.

A very desirable Kaiser is the 1949-1950 Virginian hardtop.

1949 Kaisers are facelifted

to compete with all-new rivals from the 'Big Three.' Production totals 101,000. Around 20,000 cars remain unsold and are re-sold as 1950 models.

Kaiser's last car was the two-seater Darrin.

1951 In March, a radically

restyled Kaiser arrives. It is offered in two-door as well as four-door forms. Sales rocket to 139,452.

1954 Lacking a V8, Kaiser fits

a McCulloch supercharger to the L-head six, boosting power to 140 bhp on the Manhattan. The firm also merges with Willys-Overland.

1955 Kaiser stops building

cars, having lost $100 million in 10 years.

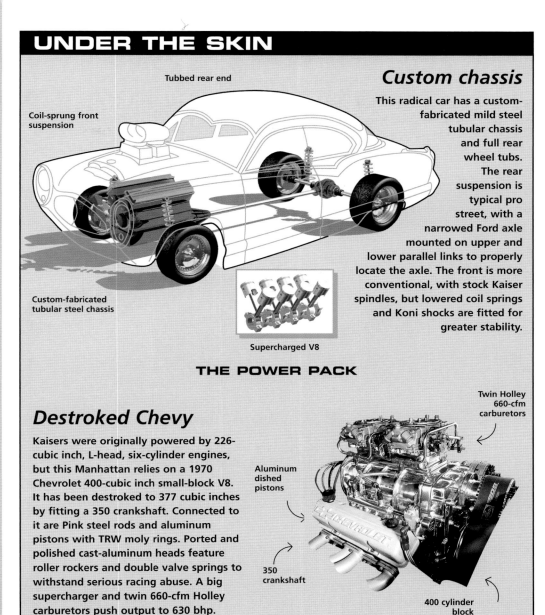

Tubbed rear end

Coil-sprung front suspension

Custom-fabricated tubular steel chassis

Supercharged V8

Custom chassis

This radical car has a custom-fabricated mild steel tubular chassis and full rear wheel tubs. The rear suspension is typical pro street, with a narrowed Ford axle mounted on upper and lower parallel links to properly locate the axle. The front is more conventional, with stock Kaiser spindles, but lowered coil springs and Koni shocks are fitted for greater stability.

THE POWER PACK

Destroked Chevy

Kaisers were originally powered by 226-cubic inch, L-head, six-cylinder engines, but this Manhattan relies on a 1970 Chevrolet 400-cubic inch small-block V8. It has been destroked to 377 cubic inches by fitting a 350 crankshaft. Connected to it are Pink steel rods and aluminum pistons with TRW moly rings. Ported and polished cast-aluminum heads feature roller rockers and double valve springs to withstand serious racing abuse. A big supercharger and twin 660-cfm Holley carburetors push output to 630 bhp.

Twin Holley 660-cfm carburetors

Aluminum dished pistons

350 crankshaft

400 cylinder block

Offbeat

Kaisers are very rare and are more often restored to stock than turned into pro-streeters. However, striking styling and a stiff structure make them ideal for custom projects. A worked small-block tubbed rear end and roll cage make 10-second ETs easily possible.

A pro street Kaiser like this makes a unique automotive statement.

Kaiser **MANHATTAN**

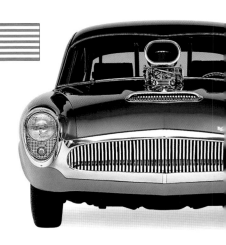

With a fortified Chevy V8, radical chassis modifications and elegant styling, customs don't come any more exclusive than this Kaiser. Best of all, it can cover 0-60 mph in just over 3 seconds.

Worked mouse

The most popular engine among hot rodders is the small-block Chevy. Nestling between the framerails of this Kaiser is a 400 motor, destroked to 377 cubic inches. With custom-machined heads, aluminum pistons, a high-lift camshaft, twin Holley carburetors and a supercharger, this Kaiser can achieve 9.8-second ¼-mile times.

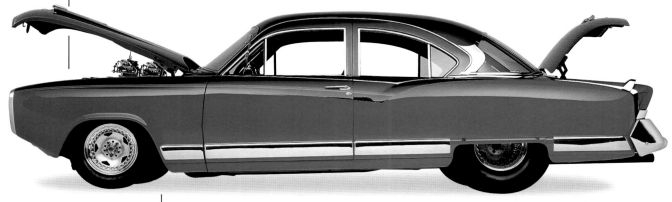

Automatic transmission

In the past, most drivers who ran their cars at the strip preferred manual transmissions, but, today, automatic units can provide more precise shifting, shaving a few tenths of a second off the ET (elapsed time). This one has a rugged GM TurboHydramatic 350 three-speed with a Hurst quarter shifter.

Radical rear end

On pro street cars, builders fill the rear fenderwells with as much rubber as possible. In order to achieve this, the rear subframe has been narrowed, Alston full wheel tubs has been welded on and a narrowed rear axle on upper and lower parallel links fitted. The 9-inch Ford differential has a Detroit Locker limited-slip differential with low 4.86:1 gears.

Low beltline

When the facelifted Kaiser was revealed in 1951, it boasted a lower beltline than contemporary Detroit sedans and more glass for greater visibility. Changes for 1954 included a concave grill, inspired by Harley Earl's Buick XP 300, and larger taillights. Two-door Manhattans, like this one, represent just five percent of 1954 production.

Custom-fabricated chassis

This Kaiser Manhattan came from the factory with a steel box-section chassis. This has been replaced with a tubular racing-style frame with a steel integral roll cage.

Sumptuous interior

Besides the customary full set of Auto Meter gauges, this Manhattan has a Budnik steering wheel, pink and purple tweed upholstery, custom front sport bucket seats and an Alpine stereo with compact disc player and amplifier.

Specifications

1954 Kaiser Manhattan

ENGINE

Type: V8

Construction: Cast-iron block and aluminum cylinder heads

Valve gear: Two valves per cylinder operated by a single camshaft with pushrods and rockers

Bore and stroke: 4.13 in. x 3.48 in.

Displacement: 377 c.i.

Compression ratio: 7.6:1

Induction system: Two Holley four-barrel carburetors and roots style supercharger

Maximum power: 630 bhp at 6,400 rpm

Maximum torque: 335 lb-ft at 4,200 rpm

Top speed: 167 mph

0-60 mph: 3.2 sec.

TRANSMISSION

GM TurboHydramatic three-speed automatic

BODY/CHASSIS

Steel tubular chassis with steel two-door sedan body

SPECIAL FEATURES

Kaiser was the first manufacturer to adopt dual-purpose taillights.

A 671 supercharger and twin 660-cfm carburetors sit atop the Chevy V8.

RUNNING GEAR

Steering: Recirculating ball

Front suspension: Unequal length A-arms with coil springs and telescopic shock absorbers

Rear suspension: Narrowed live axle mounted on upper and lower parallel links with coil springs and telescopic shock absorbers

Brakes: Drums (front and rear)

Wheels: Centerline Convo Pro, 4 x 15 in. (front), 15 x 15 in. (rear)

Tires: Mickey Thompson, 7.50 x 15 in. (front), 5 x 15 in. (rear)

DIMENSIONS

Length: 201.8 in.   **Width:** 73.2 in.

Height: 55.7 in.   **Wheelbase:** 118.5 in.

Track: 55.0 in. (front), 48.1 in. (rear)

Weight: 3,330 lbs.

Mercury LEAD SLED

In the late 1950s lowered, nosed, decked and shaved cars with chopped tops were known as lead sleds. They were a popular part of American car culture, and still are today. This radical 1949 Mercury is one of the finest around.

"...style is everything."

"When you climb into this rolling juke box the whole car seems to engulf you. It becomes apparent that styling is everything. The windows appear as tiny slits because the roof pillars have been shortened, bringing the roofline closer to the car's body. The interior sings with originality with its custom upholstery, billet knobs and late-model steering column. This heavily modified Merc isn't much of a street racer but it sure is fun to cruise in."

The custom upholstery in this wild Merc is just as ourageous as the exterior.

Milestones

1949 A radically new Mercury, with smoother Lincoln-type styling and a completely re-engineered chassis including independent suspension, helps to make its appearance. Power is still provided by the venerable 'flathead' V8.

Until 1949, Mercury's cars were essentially little more than rehashed pre-war designs.

1950 No changes this year, although a new entry-level model and a special limited edition coupe, the Monterey, join the line up. Nearly 294,000 Mercurys are sold.

The 1949-1951 Mercury was a far more modern design.

1951 The Mercury receives another facelift with more upright rear fenders and larger headlights and tail lights. A three-speed automatic transmission becomes available.

UNDER THE SKIN

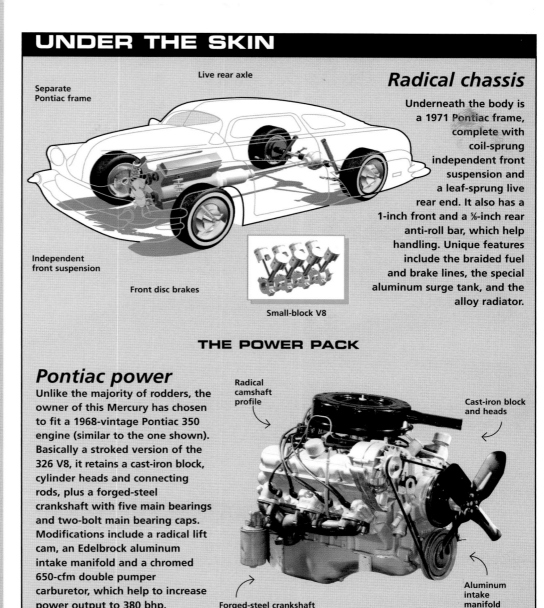

Separate Pontiac frame

Live rear axle

Independent front suspension

Front disc brakes

Small-block V8

Radical chassis

Underneath the body is a 1971 Pontiac frame, complete with coil-sprung independent front suspension and a leaf-sprung live rear end. It also has a 1-inch front and a ⅝-inch rear anti-roll bar, which help handling. Unique features include the braided fuel and brake lines, the special aluminum surge tank, and the alloy radiator.

THE POWER PACK

Pontiac power

Unlike the majority of rodders, the owner of this Mercury has chosen to fit a 1968-vintage Pontiac 350 engine (similar to the one shown). Basically a stroked version of the 326 V8, it retains a cast-iron block, cylinder heads and connecting rods, plus a forged-steel crankshaft with five main bearings and two-bolt main bearing caps. Modifications include a radical lift cam, an Edelbrock aluminum intake manifold and a chromed 650-cfm double pumper carburetor, which help to increase power output to 380 bhp.

Radical camshaft profile

Cast-iron block and heads

Forged-steel crankshaft

Aluminum intake manifold

Rolling art

In the late 1950s, 1949-1951 Fords and Mercurys were cheap and plentiful. There were dozens of different ways to customize them with varying degrees of difficulty. From GM bumpers and a DeSoto grill to extensive metal work, this one has it all.

The custom paintwork includes 140 hand-painted flames.

Mercury LEAD SLED

This Mercury has it all: the classic appearance of a 1950s custom sled, the reliability and brute power of early 1970s mechanicals and the comfort of 1990s interior fittings.

Fabricated front metal work

Like many customized Mercury's, this one has been 'nosed and decked,' which simply means that all of the chrome trim has been removed and the holes were filled in with lead. The surfaced was smoothed and painted, leaving no indication that there was ever any trim in the first place. The hood and fenders have also been reworked to make the hood opening more rounded.

Pontiac V8

Taken from a 1968 Pontiac Le Mans, the 350-cubic inch V8 has a new intake manifold and an aggressive camshaft. It makes 380 bhp and 380 lb-ft of torque, more than enough to make this car really move.

Chopped top

This Mercury has been 'chopped'—its window pillars have been cut down bringing the roof closer to the body. This modification reduces the car's overall height by a few inches and is also makes the windows look like tiny slits.

GM chassis

Although it has a Mercury body, underneath it is almost totally Pontiac, with a full-size Pontiac frame and front and rear suspension.

Shaved doors

The door handles and locks have been removed and the existing holes filled with lead. Like on the hood, the lead work is smoothed and painted. The doors are now opened using an electronic device.

Rear wheel skirts

The large wheel coverings give the Mercury a more streamlined look, but can easily be removed to change a flat tire or any other rear wheel maintenance.

Custom paint

Several coats of purple were applied to the entire car. Following the purple, custom flames were added to the nose then the Mercury received wild pinstriping to accentuate its outrageous body modifications.

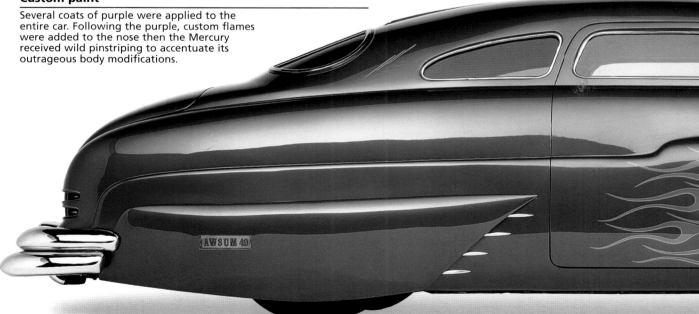

Custom fit grill

The stock grill has been removed and replaced with one from a 1954 DeSoto. The factory-installed bumper has also been shelved in favor of a modified 1957 Chevy part.

Frenched headlights

The headlight bezels were originally chrome but they have since been 'frenched.' This is a very subtle modification where the bezels are welded to the fender, smoothed, sanded and painted for a sleeker look.

Specifications

1949 Mercury Lead Sled

ENGINE

Type: V8

Construction: Cast-iron block and heads

Valve gear: Two valves per cylinder operated by pushrods and rockers

Bore and stroke: 3.89 in. x 3.75 in.

Displacement: 350 c.i.

Compression ratio: 10.5:1

Induction system: Single Holley four-barrel downdraft carburetor

Maximum power: 380 bhp at 5,100 rpm

Maximum torque: 380 lb-ft at 3,200 rpm

Top speed: 120 mph

0-60 mph: 7.8 sec.

TRANSMISSION

GM TurboHydramatic 350 with 2,500-rpm stall torque converter

BODY/CHASSIS

Steel and aluminum coupe body on separate Pontiac sub-frame

SPECIAL FEATURES

In true 1950s style, this car has twin Appleton spotlights.

Two sets of 1955 Pontiac bumpers give the rear a waterfall effect.

RUNNING GEAR

Steering: Recirculating ball

Front suspension: Unequal length wishbones with coil springs and telescopic shocks

Rear suspension: Live rear axle with leaf springs and telescopic shocks

Brakes: Discs (front), drums (rear)

Wheels: 5 x 14 in., with custom trims

Tires: Marshall whitewalls, 14 in. dia.

DIMENSIONS

Length: 200 in.   **Width:** 73 in.

Height: 51.6 in.   **Wheelbase:** 124 in.

Track: 59.1 in. (front), 62.1 in. (rear)

Weight: 3,374 lbs.

Mercury MONTCLAIR

When most people think of Mercury customs, the 1949-1951 models come to mind. However, this unusual and individual 1955 Montclair illustrates that the later Mercurys have just as much potential for customizing into one-of-a-kind vehicles.

"...a comfortable ride."

"The blue dashboard and white tuck-and-roll upholstery evoke a feeling of spaciousness. Take your place on the comfortable bench seat and start the motor. On the highway the torquey V8 enables the Mercury to do better than just keep up with the traffic and the automatic transmission is perfectly suited to laid-back cruising. The air suspension also results in a more comfortable ride than that felt in many modern cars."

This 1955 Montclair has a number of period touches, like the tuck-and-roll upholstery.

Milestones

1954 Mercury introduces
its revolutionary Y-block V8 engine. Created in response to the modern GM V8s, it features overhead valves and produces 161 bhp, making for the fastest accelerating Mercurys yet seen.

Earlier model Mercurys are popular cars to customize.

1955 Retaining the basic
1952 bodyshell, this year's Mercury has more angular styling and greater expanses of chrome. A new Montclair is introduced as the top-of-the-range model.

Mercurys were entirely redesigned for the 1957 model year. This is a top-of-the-line Turnpike Cruiser.

1956 Having proved a success,
the 1955 model receives a minor styling update. The Montclair returns and a four-door model is added to the range. An all-new Mercury debuts for 1957.

UNDER THE SKIN

Updated

In Detroit during the 1950s most cars featured a separate chassis and the 1955 Mercury was no exception. This car has been modified with an independent front suspension and a live rear axle taken from a 1981 Camaro. It also has airbags in place of the standard coil springs, and power front disc brakes are an additional safety feature.

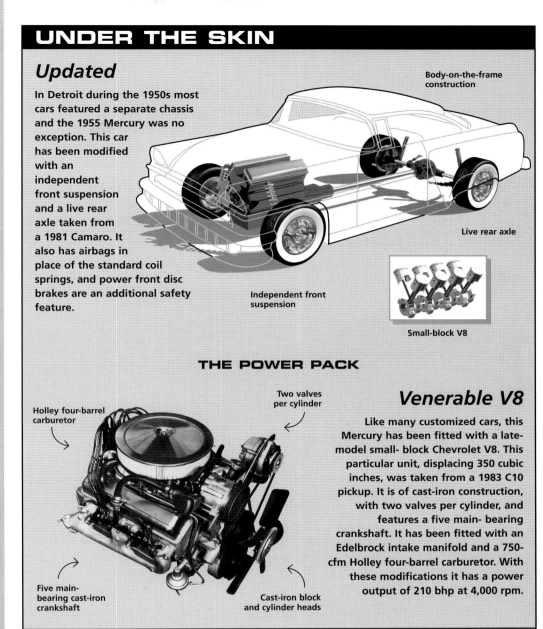

Body-on-the-frame construction

Live rear axle

Independent front suspension

Small-block V8

THE POWER PACK

Holley four-barrel carburetor

Two valves per cylinder

Five main-bearing cast-iron crankshaft

Cast-iron block and cylinder heads

Venerable V8

Like many customized cars, this Mercury has been fitted with a late-model small-block Chevrolet V8. This particular unit, displacing 350 cubic inches, was taken from a 1983 C10 pickup. It is of cast-iron construction, with two valves per cylinder, and features a five main-bearing crankshaft. It has been fitted with an Edelbrock intake manifold and a 750-cfm Holley four-barrel carburetor. With these modifications it has a power output of 210 bhp at 4,000 rpm.

Top model

In 1955 the Montclair Sun Valley hardtop coupe was the top-of-the-range Mercury. Today, most of these cars are restored to stock specifications and, therefore, a custom version makes an interesting alternative to the popular 1949-1951 Mercurys.

The Montclair makes an interesting choice for a modern custom.

Mercury **MONTCLAIR**

The Montclair Sun Valley was eye-catching when it first appeared in the mid-1950s. And with its chopped roof and custom paint, this customized Mercury continues to make a statement wherever it goes.

Chevrolet V8 engine
For practicality and power output this Mercury has a small-block Chevrolet V8 installed in place of the original Y-block engine.

Tuck-and-roll upholstery
Despite the engine and running gear this car has a number of period custom features, including the 1950s-style tuck-and-roll upholstery.

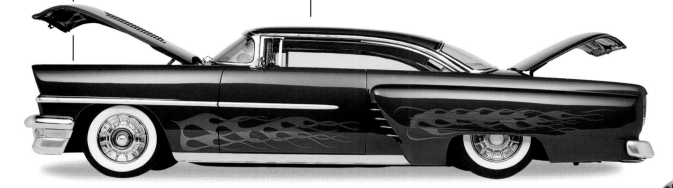

Modern running gear
A Camaro front subframe and suspension have been grafted onto the original chassis. The Salisbury rear axle was also taken from the same Camaro.

Smoothed body
Like most lead sleds the body has been smoothed out, with the headlights and taillights frenched into the body. The door handles and exterior badging have also been removed.

Air suspension
Air bags on the rear suspension give a smooth ride and also allow the car to be raised for driving or lowered for show purposes.

Modified grill

Although not obvious at first, the original bumper/grill has been reworked with additional chromed teeth.

Custom paint

As this car is driven regularly, the body has been coated in tough PPG blue acrylic urethane metallic paint. In true 1950s style, flames have been added below the beltline.

Specifications

1955 Mercury Montclair

ENGINE

Type: V8

Construction: Cast-iron block and heads

Valve gear: Two valves per cylinder operated by pushrods and rockers

Bore and stroke: 4 in. x 3.48 in.

Displacement: 350 c.i.

Compression ratio: 9.5:1

Induction system: Single Holley four-barrel carburetor

Maximum power: 210 bhp at 4,000 rpm

Maximum torque: 285 lb-ft at 2,800 rpm

Top speed: 120 mph

0-60 mph: 9.3 sec.

TRANSMISSION

Three-speed GM TurboHydramatic

BODY/CHASSIS

Separate chassis with two-door steel hardtop body

SPECIAL FEATURES

In popular lead sled style, even the radio antenna has been frenched into the bodywork.

There is even a pair of fuzzy dice hanging from the rear-view mirror—a very period custom accessory.

RUNNING GEAR

Steering: Recirculating ball

Front suspension: Independent with unequal length wishbones, air bags, front stabilizer bar and telescopic shocks

Rear suspension: Live rear axle with airbags and telescopic shocks

Brakes: Power discs, 9.5-in. dia. (front), drums, 9-in. dia. (rear)

Wheels: Steel discs, 15-in. dia. (with 1957 Cadillac hub caps)

Tires: G78 x 15 Whitewalls

DIMENSIONS

Length: 198.6 in.   **Width:** 82.7 in.

Height: 51.8 in.   **Wheelbase:** 119 in.

Track: 62.5 in (front and rear)

Weight: 3,558 lbs.

Morris MINOR

Although it was one of post-war Britain's most popular small cars, the Morris Minor could never be described as fast or powerful. The owner of this car has sorted out any performance deficit of the original.

"...this woody really flies."

"With the interior left stock, there's little to give away the fact that this is no ordinary Minor—apart from the fact that the roof is two inches lower. Start the engine and more modifications become apparent. It's clearly not the stock 803-cc engine under the hood. A deep rumbling exhaust note from up front spells out the truth—it could only be a supercharged V8. With 300 bhp this 'woody' really flies, covering the ¼-mile in less than 14 seconds."

The floor shifter and aftermarket gauges are the only modifications to the interior.

Milestones

1948 Morris launches
the Minor MM sedan. Designed by Alec Issigonis, it has a side valve engine and is available in sedan and convertible forms.

The Minor Traveller uses a structural wood frame for the rear end.

1953 The 'woody' Traveller
station wagon version is launched. It has structural rear woodwork with aluminum body panels and a lower rear axle ratio.

The Morris Minor is regarded as one of Alec Issigonis' best designs.

1956 The Minor 1000 has a bigger
948 cc engine, a one-piece windshield and a larger rear window.

1962 The engine is enlarged
to 1,098 cc taking power from 37 bhp to 48 bhp. Production of convertible models lasts until 1969 with sedans and Travellers continuing until 1971.

UNDER THE SKIN

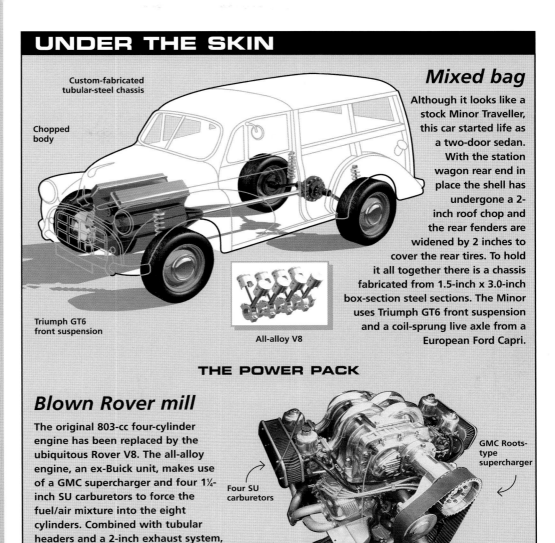

Custom-fabricated tubular-steel chassis

Chopped body

Triumph GT6 front suspension

All-alloy V8

Mixed bag

Although it looks like a stock Minor Traveller, this car started life as a two-door sedan. With the station wagon rear end in place the shell has undergone a 2-inch roof chop and the rear fenders are widened by 2 inches to cover the rear tires. To hold it all together there is a chassis fabricated from 1.5-inch x 3.0-inch box-section steel sections. The Minor uses Triumph GT6 front suspension and a coil-sprung live axle from a European Ford Capri.

THE POWER PACK

Blown Rover mill

The original 803-cc four-cylinder engine has been replaced by the ubiquitous Rover V8. The all-alloy engine, an ex-Buick unit, makes use of a GMC supercharger and four 1¼-inch SU carburetors to force the fuel/air mixture into the eight cylinders. Combined with tubular headers and a 2-inch exhaust system, the engine produces a comfortable 300 bhp. To deal with the extra heat generated there is a larger radiator and twin electric fans.

Four SU carburetors

Two valves per cylinder

GMC Roots-type supercharger

Alloy block and cylinder heads

Britain's VW

The Morris Minor is an all-time cult car and has a very strong enthusiast following. Some are even modified into street machines, although few are as unassuming, fast or tasteful as this one-off V8-powered Traveller station wagon.

Minors are cheap to buy and have great potential for hot-rodding.

Morris MINOR

Here is a car that is as happy being driven around town as it is tearing down the ¼-mile. It's got more than just speed, though, oozing that magic hot rod ingredient—old-fashioned and timeless style.

Widened rear fenders

In order to cover the wider rear wheels and tires, the rear fenders have been widened by 2 inches. This has been done so well that you'd never notice they weren't completely stock.

Roof chop

The long, low look of this car has been achieved by lowering the roof. This required cutting down all the pillars and resizing all the windows.

Sedan to wagon

This two-door sedan has been turned into a convincing (if lightly modified) 'woody' Traveller station wagon. If it wasn't a hot rod machine, this car would probably win concours competitions.

Borg-Warner transmission

To deal with so much power and torque this Morris Minor uses a Borg-Warner automatic transmission. It also benefits from a custom driveshaft and a live rear axle taken from a European 3.0-liter Ford Capri.

Well-located live axle

The live axle has AVO coil-over shock absorbers and a sturdy triangulated four-bar set up to improve axle location and reduce axle tramp.

V8 power

In place of the original 803-cc four-cylinder engine there is a Rover V8. A GMC supercharger with four SU carburetors boosts power further, giving 300 bhp and 325 lb-ft of torque.

Specifications

1953 Morris Minor

ENGINE

Type: V8

Construction: Alloy block and heads

Valve gear: Two valves per cylinder operated by a single camshaft via pushrods and rockers

Bore and stroke: 3.70 in. x 2.79 in.

Displacement: 3,950 cc

Compression ratio: 7.5:1

Induction system: GMC 471 supercharger and four SU carburetors

Maximum power: 300 bhp at 5,750 rpm

Maximum torque: 325 lb-ft at 4,300 rpm

Top speed: 125 mph

0-60 mph: 5.1 sec.

TRANSMISSION

Borg-Warner automatic

BODY/CHASSIS

Separate box-section steel chassis and steel/alloy two-door station wagon body

SPECIAL FEATURES

A V8 badge has been added below the Minor emblem and looks stock.

Early Minors have smaller grills and are preferred by collectors.

RUNNING GEAR

Steering: Rack-and-pinion

Front suspension: Double wishbones with coil springs and telescopic shock absorbers

Rear suspension: Live axle with coil springs and telescopic shock absorbers located by a triangulated four-bar set up

Brakes: Discs (front), drums (rear)

Wheels: 4.5 x 14 in. (front), 9 x 15 in. (rear)

Tires: 145/70 14 (front), 225/50 15 (rear)

DIMENSIONS

Length: 149.0 in.   **Width:** 61.0 in.

Height: 58.5 in.   **Wheelbase:** 86.0 in.

Track: 50.5 in. (front), 50.3 in. (rear)

Weight: 2,400 lbs.

Oldsmobile **88**

Compared to rival designs, the 1954-1956 Oldsmobile 88, with its relatively clean lines and panoramic front and rear windows, is one of the most attractive cars of its period.

"...as fast as a modern sedan."

"When you climb inside a car that is well over 40 years old, the last thing you expect is high performance. But, thanks to its J-2 Rocket powerplant with 312 bhp, the Oldsmobile 88 flies along. Despite its size and weight, the 88 can accelerate as fast as a modern-day performance sedan and has all the torque you'd expect from a classic V8 engine. Lowering the suspension all around has certainly helped to reduce body roll around the bends."

Base model 88s were fairly glitzy inside and two-tone was the order of the day.

Milestones

1954 New 88 series launched
on a 122-inch wheelbase in standard and Super 88 forms. A number of body styles are available: two and four-door sedan, Holiday two-door hardtop coupe and convertible.

The convertible body style was available from the start.

1955 A substantial facelift
for 1955 introduces a bold oval grill and extra two-tone paintwork options. A new two-door Holiday hardtop sedan joins the range.

By the end of the 1950s, the Oldsmobile range had much crisper styling.

1956 Another styling update
adds a 'gaping mouth' front grill and different shaped chrome side accents on the body.

1957 New Golden Rocket
models replace the existing line-up.

UNDER THE SKIN

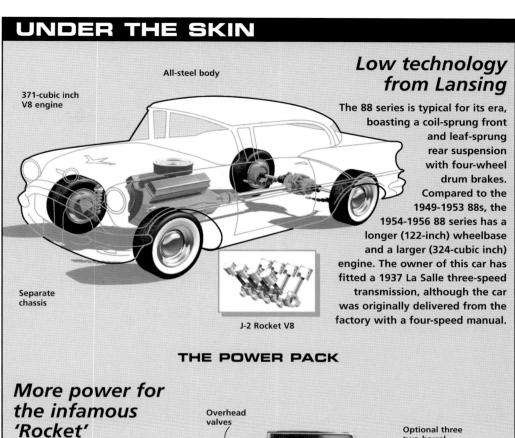

All-steel body

371-cubic inch V8 engine

Separate chassis

J-2 Rocket V8

Low technology from Lansing

The 88 series is typical for its era, boasting a coil-sprung front and leaf-sprung rear suspension with four-wheel drum brakes. Compared to the 1949-1953 88s, the 1954-1956 88 series has a longer (122-inch) wheelbase and a larger (324-cubic inch) engine. The owner of this car has fitted a 1937 La Salle three-speed transmission, although the car was originally delivered from the factory with a four-speed manual.

THE POWER PACK

More power for the infamous 'Rocket'

Based on the familiar Olds Rocket V8, the 1954 engine was bored out to 324-cubic inches and could develop between 170 and 185 bhp. This was increased to 185-202 bhp in 1955 and 230-240 bhp in 1956. The owner of this 88 has installed a 1957 371-cubic inch J-2 engine which, with its three two-barrel carburetor induction system, can produce more than 300 bhp in stock form.

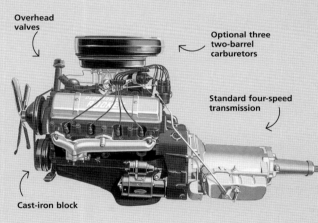

Overhead valves

Optional three two-barrel carburetors

Standard four-speed transmission

Cast-iron block

Open air

The most desirable of the 1954-1956 Oldsmobiles is the convertible. It has all the luxury and style of the sedans and hardtops, but gives the added benefit of wind-in-the-hair driving. Between 1954 and 1956, Olds built nearly 50,000 convertibles.

Classic 1950s style and a convertible top combine to make a great cruising car.

Oldsmobile 88

Between 1954 and 1957, Oldsmobile set a new production record, manufacturing some 583,000 cars in 1955 alone. Here's an example of a customized 1956.

J2 power

This car has been fitted with a 1957 371-cubic inch engine and features the J-2 option with three two-barrel carburetors. The engine has been tuned to deliver 312 bhp.

Pre-war transmission

The owner has opted to fit a vintage-style transmission from a 1937 La Salle—a prewar 'junior' Cadillac.

Lowered suspension

The suspension on this car has been lowered. At the front end, 1957 coil springs were added and cut, while lowering blocks have been mounted on the rear leaf springs.

Chrome wheels

The full chrome 7 inch x 15 inch wheels are shod with Remington tires front and rear.

Hardtop coupe style

Undoubtedly the most elegant of all the Oldsmobile 88 body variations, the Holiday hardtop coupe was also the most popular.

Thunderbird paint

Coating the body in 1990 Thunderbird Bright Red enamel paint produces a strikingly different effect and is well suited to the handsome lines on this 1956 88.

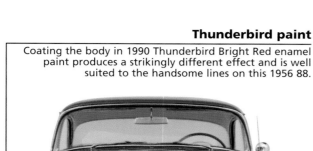

Wraparound windows

For its time, the 88 was a styling sensation, featuring sleek lines and fully wraparound glass both front and rear. The so-called Panoramic wraparound treatment was pioneered by the 1953 Oldsmobile Ninety-Eight Fiesta.

Specifications
1956 Oldsmobile 88 Holiday hardtop coupe

ENGINE

Type: V8

Construction: Cast-iron cylinder block and cylinder heads

Valve gear: Two valves per cylinder operated by single camshaft via pushrods and rockers

Bore and stroke: 4.0 in. x 3.69 in.

Displacement: 371 c.i.

Compression ratio: 8.4:1

Induction system: Three two-barrel carburetors

Maximum power: 312 bhp at 4,600 rpm

Maximum torque: 410 lb-ft at 2,800 rpm

Top speed: 121 mph

0-60 mph: 8.7 sec.

TRANSMISSION

1937 La Salle three-speed manual

BODY/CHASSIS

Steel chassis with two-door hardtop coupe body

SPECIAL FEATURES

The grill of the 1956 Oldsmobile was unique to that year, with a big divider and horizontal bars.

Outer space was a popular theme among stylists in the 1950s which is evident on this 88's taillights.

RUNNING GEAR

Steering: Recirculating ball

Front suspension: Independent with coil springs

Rear suspension: Live axle with semi-elliptic leaf springs

Brakes: Drums, front and rear

Wheels: Pressed steel, 15-in. dia.

Tires: Remington G-78 (front), L-78 (rear)

DIMENSIONS

Length: 203.4 in.   **Width:** 77 in.

Height: 60 in.   **Wheelbase:** 122 in.

Track: 59 in. (front), 58 in. (rear)

Curb weight: 3,771 lbs.

Oldsmobile **SUPER 88**

A 1949 Mercury most often springs to mind when you hear the term 'American custom.' Few would equate the term with cars such as this 1960 Oldsmobile, but this Super 88 certainly has the edge on some custom Mercs.

"...a powerful sound."

"Most of these cars came with a big front bench seat, but you won't find one in this car. Instead, it has a pair of custom buckets and a center console. Under the hood, the worked 350— coupled to a TurboHydramatic—emits a powerful sound and has enough grunt to move the 3,860-lbs. This Olds can reach 60 mph in less than 9 seconds. A soft highway ride gives the sensation of floating on air, but the best part is that with this car, you never fail to attract attention."

The original dashboard and steering wheel mate well with the custom seats and console.

Milestones

1958 After the
1958 models, Oldsmobile reveals its dramatically restyled 1959 cars. These are built off new body platforms and are much lower, longer and sleeker. The range is divided into Dynamic, Super 88, and top-of-the-line, the Ninety-Eight. Engines range from a 270-bhp 371 V8 to a new 394 packing an awesome 300 bhp.

The sportiest Olds of the early 1960s was the Starfire.

1959 Late in the
year, the unchanged 1960 models are released. Styling is toned down slightly, but sales remain strong—over 347,000 cars are built.

The 88 name was still going strong in 1999.

1961 Shorter and
narrower bodies are new for the big 1961 Oldsmobiles, as is the advent of a new series.

UNDER THE SKIN

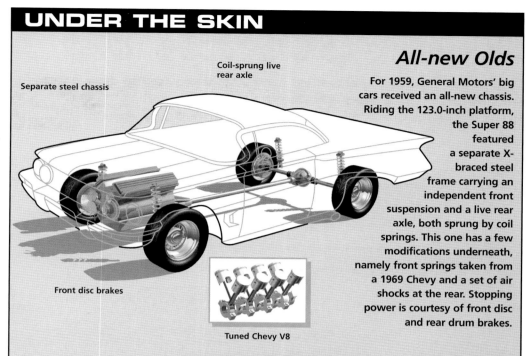

Coil-sprung live rear axle

Separate steel chassis

Front disc brakes

Tuned Chevy V8

All-new Olds

For 1959, General Motors' big cars received an all-new chassis. Riding the 123.0-inch platform, the Super 88 featured a separate X-braced steel frame carrying an independent front suspension and a live rear axle, both sprung by coil springs. This one has a few modifications underneath, namely front springs taken from a 1969 Chevy and a set of air shocks at the rear. Stopping power is courtesy of front disc and rear drum brakes.

THE POWER PACK

The general's Brethren

Like other GM divisions in the 1950s and 1960s, Oldsmobile built its own engines. The standard in the 1960 Super 88 series was a 394-cubic inch big-block with 315 bhp. Under the hood of this one, however, lurks a slightly different motor—a 350-cubic inch Chevy V8. It has a cast-iron block with aluminum-alloy cylinder heads, a roller camshaft, forged-steel crankshaft and forged pistons, and high-flow valves. Topped by an Edelbrock 650-cfm four-barrel carburetor, the small-block pumps out a respectable 345 bhp—good enough for 0-60 times of 8.3 seconds.

Scenic rod

Of over 347,000 Oldsmobiles built for 1960, only 16,464 were Super 88 hardtop coupes. These use Olds' biggest V8 that year—a 394—and look good, both stock or custom. Good examples can be picked up for reasonable amounts.

A short chassis with the biggest engine—the Super 88 was the Olds hot rod.

Oldsmobile SUPER 88

Back in the Eisenhower era, most American cars were big. Size is not the only factor that makes this Super 88 a knockout. It also boasts eye-catching looks, sumptuous comfort and healthy V8 power.

Chevrolet V8 engine

It left the factory with a torquey 394, but the original motor has been replaced by a small-block Chevy, for reasons of cost and practicality. The modified and fully balanced motor cranks out 345 bhp, thanks to aluminum heads, an Edelbrock four-barrel carburetor and other enhancements.

Coil-sprung rear end

Like its GM siblings, the 1960 Olds runs on an all-coil-sprung suspension, with unequal-length A-arms at the front and a live axle at the rear. The setup on this car is more or less stock, with the exception of 1969 Chevy front springs and custom air shocks out back.

X-braced chassis

Like the 1959 models, the 1960 Oldsmobiles retained an X-braced chassis frame, offered in two different forms. The Dynamic and Super 88 models have 123 inches between the wheel centers, while the Ninety-Eight has a longer, 126.3-inch wheelbase frame.

Two-door hardtop styling

Both the Dynamic and Super 88 hardtops are called Scenic coupes, and with a wraparound windshield and bubble backlight, visibility is certainly excellent. This bodystyle is quite rare— fewer than 46,000 were built for 1960.

Body modifications

Many of the custom touches on this car are subtle. The hood has been extended and peaked by 2 inches for a more exaggerated look, the taillights frenched, the door handles and locks were shaved and fender extractors from a 1970s Trans Am added.

1960 Oldsmobile Super 88

ENGINE

Type: V8

Construction: Cast-iron block and alloy heads

Valve gear: Two valves per cylinder operated by a single V-mounted camshaft with pushrods and rockers

Bore and stroke: 4.00 in. x 3.48 in.

Displacement: 350 c.i.

Compression ratio: 8.5:1

Induction system: Edelbrock 650-cfm four-barrel carburetor

Maximum power: 345 bhp at 5,800 rpm

Maximum torque: 370 lb-ft at 3,000 rpm

Top speed: 120 mph

0-60 mph: 8.3 sec.

TRANSMISSION

TH400 three-speed automatic

BODY/CHASSIS

Separate steel chassis with two-door hardtop body

SPECIAL FEATURES

Attention to detail is highlighted in the radio antenna, which has been frenched into the body.

Sidepipes are standard for any 1960s-style custom.

RUNNING GEAR

Steering: Recirculating-ball

Front suspension: Unequal-length A-arms with coil springs, telescopic shock absorbers and anti-roll bar

Rear suspension: Live axle with semi-trailing arms, coil springs and telescopic shock absorbers

Brakes: Discs (front), drums (rear)

Wheels: KMC chrome reverse, 8 x 15 in.

Tires: Cooper Cobra GTS, P255/60 R15

DIMENSIONS

Length: 217.6 in.   **Width:** 89.8 in.

Height: 56.1 in.   **Wheelbase:** 123.0 in.

Track: 61.0 in. (front and rear)

Weight: 3,860 lbs.

Plymouth FURY

Few street-driven cars are as radical as this 1957 Fury, with its blown race Hemi and outlandish appearance. In fact, this car gained so much attention that it has been replicated by Hot Wheels as a 1:48 scale model.

"...well-harnessed power."

"Start up the blown Hemi and just listen to the sound—it's enough to make anyone weak at the knees. With a TorqueFlite transmission and monster rear tires, the power is well harnessed. Even though the car goes ballistic once the accelerator hits the floor, it feels stable and controllable, a trait seldom found in such high-horsepower street machines. With overdrive, premium shocks and a comfortable driver's seat, it is also good for summertime cruising."

Inside, this Fury appears surprisingly stock with full trim and carpeting.

Milestones

1956 Arriving halfway through the
model year, the Fury is a limited production special, with a four-barrel 303-cubic inch V8 and white paint with gold anodized accents.

The Fury gained a 318-cubic inch V8 for 1957.

1957 Radically reworked with modern
styling, Plymouth has a banner year, with over 762,000 built. Furys return, still only as hardtops, packing a 290-bhp 318 Wedgehead V8.

The Fury's counterpart at Dodge was the D-500; this is a 1958 model.

1958 The Fury gets twin headlights, plus
revised bumpers, grill and taillight assembly. A 350-cubic inch engine with up to 315 bhp joins the 318 as a Fury option.

1959 A new Sport Fury convertible is offered
alongside the hardtop.

UNDER THE SKIN

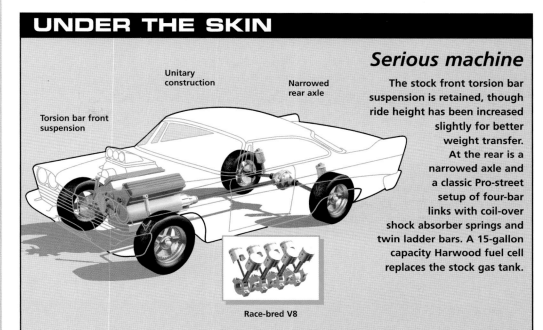

Unitary construction

Narrowed rear axle

Torsion bar front suspension

Race-bred V8

Serious machine

The stock front torsion bar suspension is retained, though ride height has been increased slightly for better weight transfer. At the rear is a narrowed axle and a classic Pro-street setup of four-bar links with coil-over shock absorber springs and twin ladder bars. A 15-gallon capacity Harwood fuel cell replaces the stock gas tank.

THE POWER PACK

Overkill Hemi

Furys were among the hottest Detroit cars of their day, but this particular one ranks as one of the hottest street machines of all time. Sitting between the fenders is a 1971-vintage 426-cubic inch Hemi V8 in place of the standard 318-cubic inch powerplant. A serious performance piece, it has been overbored to 511 cubic inches and fitted with a Keith Black stroker crankshaft, KB aluminum pistons and con rods, polished and ported heads, a B.D.S. supercharger nestled on Hilborn four-port injectors, a Cragar 'bird-catcher' intake and a large, wet nitrous system.

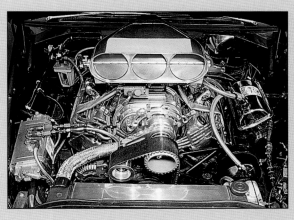

Rare potential

Not many cars are as dramatic or memorable as the late-1950s Fury, but low production numbers (only 7,483 were built for 1957) and rust problems make these cars a rarity today. However, as a potential street machine the Fury is difficult to beat.

Alternative yes, but few cars attract attention like a modified Fury.

Plymouth FURY

Fast and flamboyant, even in 1957, the Plymouth Fury is high on style and power. It is also different, and crafting one into a pro-streeter is guaranteed to gain attention anywhere.

Famous racing V8

Before being installed in this Fury, the 1971-vintage Hemi V8 powered Parnelli Jones' famous Vels Plymouth Cuda funny car. The only changes are a milder cam and Hilborn intake to make it more streetable.

Torsion bar suspension

In addition to new styling, 1957 also marked the debut of torsion bar front suspension on Plymouths. One advantage is that they can be easily cranked to raise or lower ride height for better handling or weight transfer.

Custom exhaust

Helping the engine produce its astonishing power are 2¼-inch custom-fabricated exhaust headers. Exhaust gases exit ahead of the rear axle.

Narrowed rear

Maximum acceleration is what this car is all about, and aiding this is a narrowed Sutton Engineering unit with a set of 5:13 cogs. Huge 15-inch slicks and ladder bars help the car bite.

Forward styling

Plymouth ads claimed 'suddenly it's 1960' and compared to rival cars the 1957 range seemed three years ahead, thanks to a low belt line and large blade-like fins. This was arguably the finest hour for Virgil Exner styling.

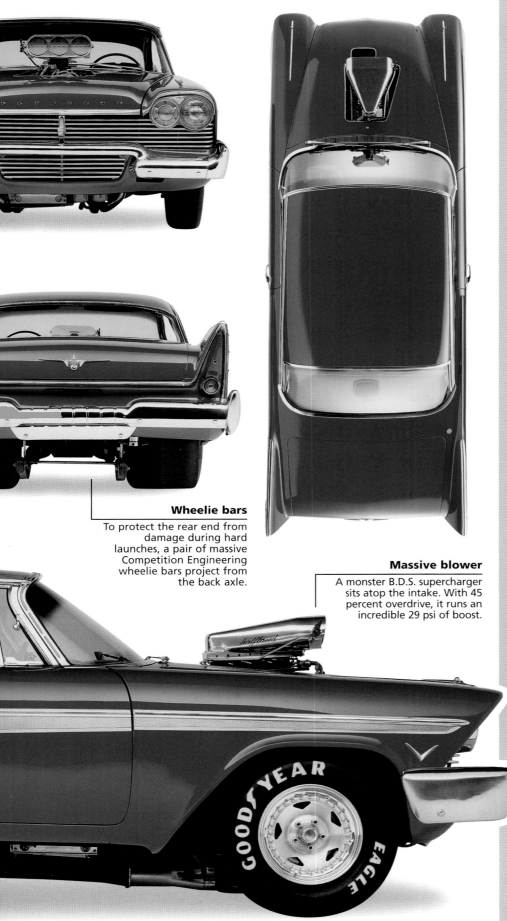

Specifications

1957 Plymouth Fury

ENGINE

Type: V8

Construction: Cast-iron block and heads

Valve gear: Two valves per cylinder operated by pushrods and roller valve lifters

Bore and stroke: 4.85 in. x 3.75 in.

Displacement: 511 c.i.

Compression ratio: 10.0:1

Induction system: Hilborn mechanical four-port fuel injection

Maximum power: 1,485 bhp at 7,200 rpm

Maximum torque: 1,250 lb-ft at 4,200 rpm

Top speed: 197 mph

0-60 mph: 2.6 sec..

TRANSMISSION

TorqueFlite 727 three-speed automatic

BODY/CHASSIS

Separate steel chassis with two-door coupe body

SPECIAL FEATURES

Push-button transmission controls were offered on Chryslers in the late 1950s.

Even though this is a serious street machine, it still has a stereo and retractable fender-mounted antenna.

RUNNING GEAR

Steering: Recirculating ball

Front suspension: Unequal-length A-arms with torsion bars and telescopic shock absorbers

Rear suspension: Live rear axle with upper and lower parallel links, coil springs and telescopic shock absorbers

Brakes: Discs (front and rear)

Wheels: Convo, 7 x 15 in. (front), 15 x 15 in. (rear)

Tires: Goodyear Eagle, 15-in. slicks

DIMENSIONS

Length: 205.0 in. **Width:** 78.0 in.

Height: 57.0 in.   **Wheelbase:** 118.0 in.

Track: 59.8 in. (front), 45.2 in. (rear)

Weight: 3,520 lbs.

Wheelie bars
To protect the rear end from damage during hard launches, a pair of massive Competition Engineering wheelie bars project from the back axle.

Massive blower
A monster B.D.S. supercharger sits atop the intake. With 45 percent overdrive, it runs an incredible 29 psi of boost.

Plymouth ROAD RUNNER

Less powerful and more portly than its illustrious predecessors, the 1973 Road Runner is not particularly coveted, but all the basics are in place to turn it into a serious street machine.

"...bad boy, all-American."

"The Tuff steering wheel is still there, but the auxiliary gauges, roll cage and harness tell you that this is no luke-warm, stock 1973 Road Runner. A bored-out 440 under the multi-scooped hood and 4.56 gears in the rear end translate into astonishing acceleration once you hit the pedal. The big tires hook up instantly, and the roar from the exhaust delivers a sound that could only come from a bad boy, all-American street racer."

A SCS Cheetah floor shift helps the driver to get the most from the 727 transmission.

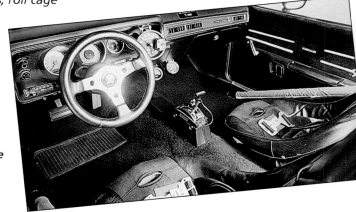

Milestones

1968 Plymouth
introduces a budget no-frills muscle car that is tied in with the Warner Brothers cartoon character of the same name (the horn even makes the beep-beep sound). It is an unexpected hit, selling nearly 45,000 in its first year.

The Road Runner debuted as a 1968 model with a standard 383-cubic inch V8.

1971 A second-
generation Road Runner with a shorter fuselage-style body and wider track arrives. It is offered only in hardtop coupe form.

The wildest of all Road Runners was the 1970 Superbird.

1972 The Hemi is
dropped, but a GTX option on the Road Runner adds the 440, now rated at 280 bhp.

1974 A fuel crisis
spells the end of the Road Runner. There are 11,555 built in the final year.

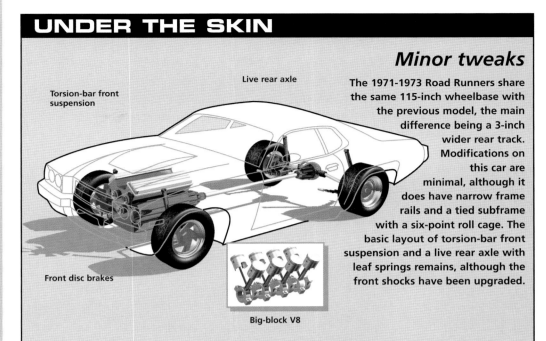

Torsion-bar front suspension

Live rear axle

Front disc brakes

Big-block V8

Minor tweaks

The 1971-1973 Road Runners share the same 115-inch wheelbase with the previous model, the main difference being a 3-inch wider rear track. Modifications on this car are minimal, although it does have narrow frame rails and a tied subframe with a six-point roll cage. The basic layout of torsion-bar front suspension and a live rear axle with leaf springs remains, although the front shocks have been upgraded.

THE POWER PACK

MOPAR Madness

Engines available in the stock 1973 Road Runner ranged from a 340 four-barrel small-block V8 to 400 and 440 big-blocks. This car is powered by a 440 but it has slightly more than 285 emissions-choked horsepower. It has been overbored by .030 inches resulting in a displacement of 446 cubic inches. It has stronger Six-Pack connecting rods, 8.0:1 compression pistons, a fully balanced rotating assembly, a special Offenhauser intake manifold with dual Edelbrock Competition four-barrel carburetors, plus a pair of 2.25-inch primary Hooker exhaust headers. This contributes to a power output of 430 bhp at 6,200 rpm.

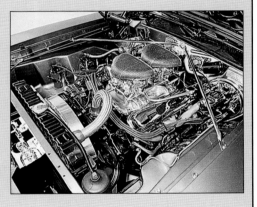

Street heat

In stock form, a 1973 Road Runner is not a particularly quick car, but its torsion-bar front suspension, unitary chassis and room for big-block power single out its potential for street-machine duty. Best of all, these cars can be picked up for pocket change.

Fat rear tires, fancy paint and a built 440 make for one cool street machine.

Plymouth ROAD RUNNER

One of the last holdouts of the muscle era, this 1973 Road Runner has been immortalized by the addition of a big-inch modified motor, a stiffened chassis and a healthy dose of MOPAR madness.

Big, bad 440
MOPAR's largest V8 of the early 1970s lies under the massive hood. Fully balanced and blueprinted, it whips out 430 bhp and an incredible 515 lb-ft of torque.

Metallic paint
Adding a modern touch to the curvy 1970s sheetmetal is Deltron Silver Frost metallic paint, set off by garish side graphics.

Big meats
To get the best acceleration possible, massive 15 x 14-inch Weld billet rims have been fitted at the rear. These are shod with sticky Mickey Thompson 31 x 18.5 tires.

Adjustable shocks

Koni tube shock absorbers have been fitted at the front. They are both stiffer yet easier to adjust than the stock shocks.

Custom interior

Black JAZ bucket seats and black carpeting combine to create a stark interior in this Road Runner.

Racing transmission

Even in stock form, the 727 TorqueFlite is a drag racer's favorite. This one is built by Cledus and includes an SCS Cheetah floor shifter.

Specifications

1973 Plymouth Road Runner

ENGINE

Type: V8

Construction: Cast-iron block and heads

Valve gear: Two valves per cylinder operated by a single V-mounted camshaft via pushrods and rockers

Bore and stroke: 4.65 in. x 3.75 in.

Displacement: 446 c.i.

Compression ratio: 8.0:1

Induction system: Two Edelbrock four-barrel carburetors

Maximum power: 430 bhp at 6,200 rpm

Maximum torque: 515 lb-ft at 3,800 rpm

Top speed: 135 mph

0-60 mph: 4.9 sec.

TRANSMISSION

TorqueFlite 727 three-speed automatic

BODY/CHASSIS

Steel unitary chassis with two-door coupe body

SPECIAL FEATURES

An SCS Cheetah shifter helps give the driver extra control over the transmission's shift points.

The bulged hood provides just enough clearance for the two four barrels.

RUNNING GEAR

Steering: Recirculating-ball

Front suspension: Upper and lower A-arms with longitudinal torsion bars, telescopic shock absorbers and anti-roll bar

Rear suspension: Live rear axle with leaf springs and telescopic shock absorbers

Brakes: Discs (front), drums (rear)

Wheels: 15 x 6 in. (front), 15 x 14 in. (rear)

Tires: Michelin P205/15 R75 (front), Mickey Thompson 31 x 18.5 (rear)

DIMENSIONS

Length: 210.8 in.   **Width:** 81.3 in.

Height: 55.7 in.   **Wheelbase:** 115.0 in.

Track: 65.8 in. (front), 56.6 in. (rear)

Weight: 3,525 lbs.

Pontiac VENTURA

Stylish, both then and now, the 1961 Ventura combines both luxury and performance. The owner of this car has chosen to upgrade its performance while retaining the Ventura's classic looks.

"...plenty of power to spare."

"With its big V8 and four-barrel carburetor, the 1961 Ventura has plenty of power to spare, taking less than seven seconds to reach 60 mph. In a straight line, the heavy Ventura can outrun plenty of modern sports cars. Around corners, though, the car shows its age. The steering is vague and there's a lot of body roll, and despite its modern tires, the back end easily breaks loose."

The dash is original, but the seats have been reupholstered for a custom look.

Milestones

1960 Pontiac introduces the Ventura nameplate as a trim level on its Catalina™ line. Two body styles, a hardtop coupe and Vista sedan, are available.

Ed 'Fireball' Roberts was a highly successful stock-car racer in early 1960s full-size Pontiacs.

1961 Slightly shorter and lighter, this year's full-size Pontiacs are established as performance cars. Pontiacs take the first three places in the NASCAR Daytona 500 Stock Car race.

Roberts won the Daytona 500 in 1962 in this Pontiac Catalina.

1962 The Ventura is dropped, although a sporty new Grand Prix™ makes its debut. It features bucket seats and a full instrumentation pack. A 389-cubic inch V8 is the only engine available.

UNDER THE SKIN

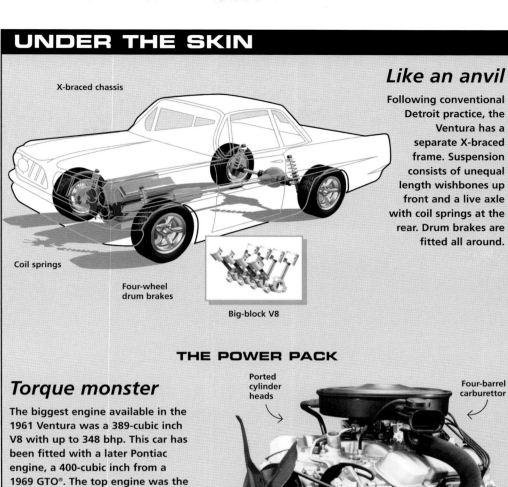

X-braced chassis

Coil springs

Four-wheel drum brakes

Big-block V8

Like an anvil

Following conventional Detroit practice, the Ventura has a separate X-braced frame. Suspension consists of unequal length wishbones up front and a live axle with coil springs at the rear. Drum brakes are fitted all around.

THE POWER PACK

Torque monster

The biggest engine available in the 1961 Ventura was a 389-cubic inch V8 with up to 348 bhp. This car has been fitted with a later Pontiac engine, a 400-cubic inch from a 1969 GTO®. The top engine was the Ram Air IV that gave 370 bhp, but the engine in this car is a tuned Ram Air III that gives more power than the radical Ram Air IV. With free-flow exhaust and ported cylinder heads, this engine makes 380 bhp. Torque has also been increased to 450 lb-ft.

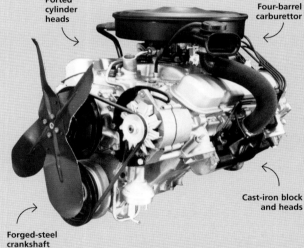

Ported cylinder heads

Four-barrel carburettor

Cast-iron block and heads

Forged-steel crankshaft

Down-sized

The 1961 Pontiacs received shorter, narrower bodies and weighed slightly less. The Ventura was based on the Catalina platform and came in just two body styles. The hardtop coupe proved to be the least popular, though 13,297 were built.

Full size and full power; this Ventura is a stunning customized street machine.

Pontiac VENTURA

Full-size early-1960s Pontiacs have a special feel about them. This Ventura, with its Tri-Power induction and Torque Thrust wheels, is straight from the muscle-car era.

Custom paint

Many customizers adopt late-model paint finishes. This Ventura has been resprayed in 1993 Ford 'Coronado Red' paint.

Racing wheels

This Pontiac has been fitted with a set of American Racing Torque Thrust wheels, a popular aftermarket item in the 1960s.

Youthful appeal

The Pontiac was emerging as a more sporty, younger person's car in the early 1960s and the Ventura was available with bucket seats and a four-speed manual transmission. This example, however, retains the traditional front bench seat.

Chrome accents

The huge chrome side spears running along the beltline are a trademark of General Motors cars from the period.

Bubble-top fastback

The 'bubble'-type rear window looks stylish and actually improved aerodynamics on the NASCAR Pontiacs.

Wide-track ride

Since 1959, the large Pontiacs adopted a wider track, helping to make them some of the most stable full-size cars of the era.

Stainless-steel exhaust

To extract maximum power, an Edelbrock stainless-steel exhaust with 2½-inch diameter pipes has been fitted.

Ram Air III engine

This particular car has a Ram Air III 400-cubic inch engine from a 1969 Pontiac GTO. Mild tuning means it gives 380 bhp.

Specifications

1961 Pontiac Ventura

ENGINE

Type: V8

Construction: Cast-iron block and heads

Valve gear: Single camshaft operated by pushrods and rockers

Bore and stroke: 4.12 in. x 3.75 in.

Displacement: 400 c.i.

Compression ratio: 10.75:1

Induction system: Single four-barrel carburetor

Maximum power: 380 bhp at 5,500 rpm

Maximum torque: 450 lb-ft at 3,900 rpm

Top speed: 124 mph

0-60 mph: 6.5 sec.

TRANSMISSION

GM TurboHydramatic 400 three-speed automatic with a 2,000-rpm stall converter

BODY/CHASSIS

Steel X-braced frame with separate two-door coupe steel body

SPECIAL FEATURES

Torque Thrust wheels add a period touch to this Ventura.

Although toned down, there is still plenty of chrome.

RUNNING GEAR

Steering: Recirculating ball with power assistance

Front suspension: Unequal length upper and lower wishbones with coil springs and telescopic shocks

Rear suspension: Live rear axle with coil springs and telescopic shocks

Brakes: Drums (front and rear)

Wheels: Cast-magnesium, 15 in.

Tyres: BF Goodrich radial T/A 215/65-15 (front), 235/75-15 (rear)

DIMENSIONS

Length: 207.8 in.   **Width:** 118.9 in.

Height: 66.1 in.   **Wheelbase:** 119 in.

Track: 61 in. (front), 59.5 in. (rear)

Weight: 3,687 lbs.

Studebaker CHAMPION

One of the most charismatic cars of the early 1950s is the Studebaker Champion coupe. Nicknamed the 'Bullet Nose,' it is the car's unusual styling that attracts customizers, who sometimes turn them into some of the most bizarre creations ever to hit the road.

"...a case of old meets new."

"Here it really is a case of old meets new. The velour door panels and modern bucket seats contrast strongly with the painted metal dash. The V8 has plenty of grunt, enabling you to pass slower traffic with ease. With its lowered stance and wide tires, this Stude is also quite at home on winding roads. Best of all, though, the styling and modifications mean that no matter where you go you are bound to attract attention."

Inside the Champion, there is little to indicate that this is a 1950s car.

Milestones

1947 Thanks to wartime preparation, Studebaker is able to launch all-new cars ahead of its rivals. Two lines are offered: the Champion and Commander.

The bullet-nose Studebaker was also available as a convertible.

1950 In order to remain competitive, the 1947 design is facelifted with a controversial bullet-type nose. A new 232-cubic inch V8 becomes optional in Commanders.

Later Studebakers were also styled by Raymond Loewy.

1951 Prices rise slightly this year and the 'bullet nose' is toned down. Government production cutbacks due to the Korean War see sales dip slightly to 246,195. The basic 1947 design continues into 1952 —its final season—without the bullet-nose front end.

UNDER THE SKIN

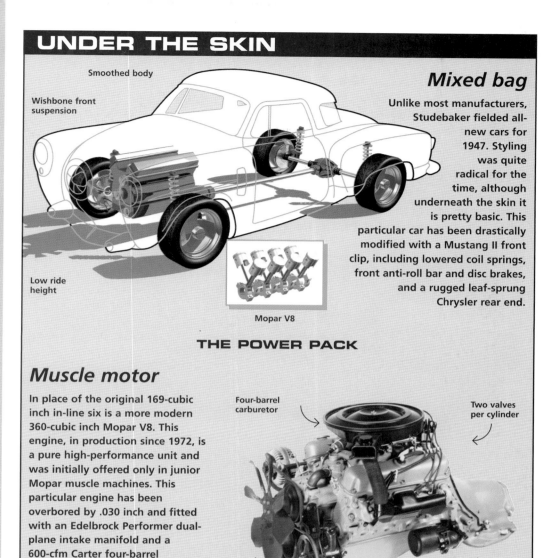

Smoothed body

Wishbone front suspension

Low ride height

Mopar V8

Mixed bag

Unlike most manufacturers, Studebaker fielded all-new cars for 1947. Styling was quite radical for the time, although underneath the skin it is pretty basic. This particular car has been drastically modified with a Mustang II front clip, including lowered coil springs, front anti-roll bar and disc brakes, and a rugged leaf-sprung Chrysler rear end.

THE POWER PACK

Muscle motor

In place of the original 169-cubic inch in-line six is a more modern 360-cubic inch Mopar V8. This engine, in production since 1972, is a pure high-performance unit and was initially offered only in junior Mopar muscle machines. This particular engine has been overbored by .030 inch and fitted with an Edelbrock Performer dual-plane intake manifold and a 600-cfm Carter four-barrel carburetor. This results in 244 bhp at 4,200 rpm and a respectable amount of torque.

Four-barrel carburetor

Two valves per cylinder

Overbored cylinders

Cast-iron block and heads

Loewy style

Not perhaps the obvious choice for a street machine, the Raymond Lowey-styled 1950-1951 Studebakers have a special quality that attracts many customizers. Plenty of these cars were built, so there is a large selection from which to choose.

Raymond Loewy's space-age styling lends itself to the custom look.

Studebaker CHACMPION

The bullet-nose Studebakers are already head-turners in stock factory form, but when they are properly modified they become crowd-stopping cars. This radical Champion is one of the finest modified Studebakers around.

V8 engine

Most people will tell you that all true hot rods have V8 engines. This Studebaker is no exception. In place of the original six is an overbored 360-cubic inch V8 taken from a 1978 Dodge Ramcharger truck. It has been mildly tweaked and produces 244 bhp.

Monochromatic paint

Some hot-rodders choose glossy, fancy paint jobs, while others go down a more conservative route. This Stude has its exterior finished in semi-gloss Tangerine Pearl and is fairly conservative.

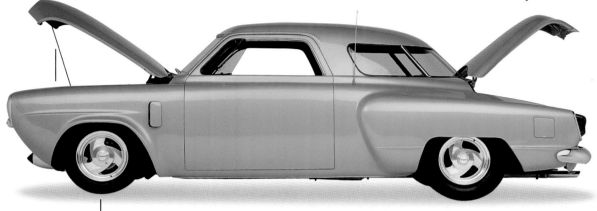

Mustang II front suspension

At the front, the original suspension has been replaced by a Mustang II front clip—a favorite for street machines. This includes the upper and lower wishbones and coil springs for an improved ride.

Automatic transmission

Backing up the torquey V8 is Chrysler's well-proven TorqueFlite 727 three-speed automatic, which has been upgraded with a shift kit to improve performance. This transmits power to a Chrysler rear end that has 3.42:1 final drive for relaxed cruising.

Wraparound rear window

The most distinctive feature after the bullet-type nose is the wraparound rear window. This was offered only on the 'Starlight' five-passenger coupes and lasted through 1952. Besides being dramatic looking, it also offers excellent rearward visibility.

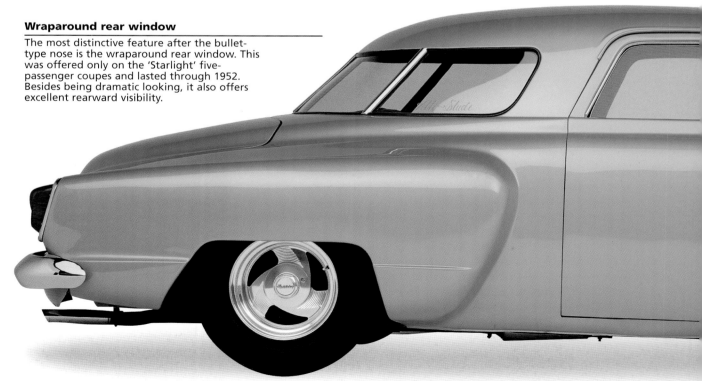

Specifications

1951 Studebaker Champion

ENGINE

Type: V8

Construction: Cast-iron block and heads

Valve gear: Two valves per cylinder operated by a single camshaft via pushrods and rockers

Bore and stroke: 4.30 in. x 3.58 in.

Displacement: 360 c.i.

Compression ratio: 8.4:1

Induction system: Four-barrel carburetor

Maximum power: 244 bhp at 4,200 rpm

Maximum torque: 290 lb-ft at 3,000 rpm

Top speed: 115 mph

0-60 mph: 9.8 sec.

TRANSMISSION

TorqueFlite three-speed automatic

BODY/CHASSIS

Steel two-door coupe on separate chassis

SPECIAL FEATURES

The car gets its 'bullet-nose' tag from this distinctive grill treatment.

Three-spoke American Eagle aluminum wheels are perfect for this car.

Body modifications

Although the exterior may look stock, it has been subjected to a few subtle changes. The rear fenderwells and wheel openings have been widened and reshaped, plus all seams have been filled and all chrome trim removed. The front has also been altered with the valance extended and 'Dagmar' front bumpers from a 1957 Cadillac fitted.

RUNNING GEAR

Steering: Recirculating ball

Front suspension: Wishbones with coil springs, telescopic shock absorbers and anti-roll bar

Rear suspension: Live axle with leaf springs and telescopic shock absorbers

Brakes: Discs (front), drums (rear)

Wheels: American Eagle, 7 x 15 in. (front), 8 x 15 in. (rear)

Tires: 215/60 15 (front), 275/60 15 (rear)

DIMENSIONS

Length: 187.5 in. **Width:** 72.0 in.

Height: 56.0 in. **Wheelbase:** 115.0 in.

Track: 62.0 in. (front), 68.5 in. (rear)

Weight: 2,690 lbs.

Volkswagen **BEETLE**

It may have been the best-selling car of the 20th century, but the Beetle is almost certainly one the most modified cars as well. Such is their popularity, modified Beetles support their own specialist industry.

"...surprising acceleration."

"The first thing that strikes you when you sit in this Beetle is the simple and uncluttered interior. The large speedometer dominates the painted metal dashboard, while the tachometer is hidden underneath it. Despite its high state of tune, the engine still has Wolfsburg's familiar flat-four exhaust note spluttering from its huge tailpipe. It has superb traction off the line and offers surprising acceleration in a most un-Beetle-like manner."

A classic wooden steering wheel really sets off the simple, uncluttered interior.

Milestones

1934 Ferdinand Porsche
presents his new 'people's car,' the KdF Wagen. Commissioned by the Nazi government, it has been tested by SS soldiers.

Friendly and unusual styling lends itself to modifications.

1945 The Allied Forces
help to restart production at the Wolfsburg factory after the war. The car is now called the Volkswagen.

1949 The first official export
Beetle rolls off the line, with the U.S. being one of the biggest markets. By the recession of the late 1950s, sales begin to rise.

There are many forms of Beetle-based motorsport.

1978 Production ends
in Germany after more than 20 million have been built. Mexican production continues.

UNDER THE SKIN

Heavy-duty Bug

The Beetle has an immensely strong rolling chassis. It is a self-contained unit with two floorpans welded to a central backbone. At the rear there is a sturdy fork where the transmission is bolted, and transverse torsion bars suspend the car. This particular car has revalved shock absorbers and bigger brakes. There is a narrowed front beam, adjustable rear springs and heavy-duty transmission mounts.

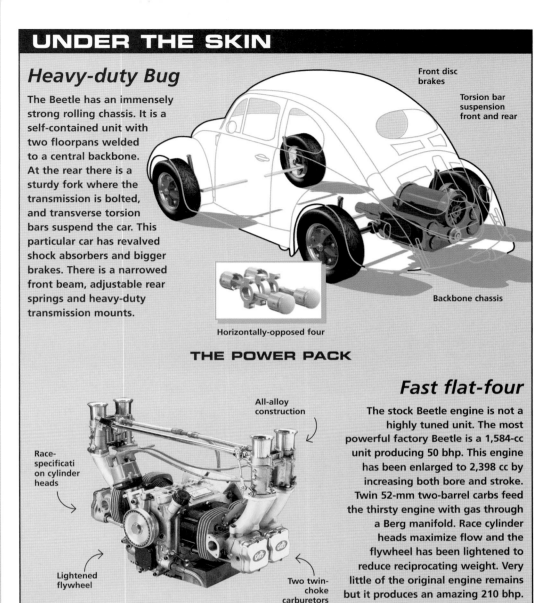

Front disc brakes

Torsion bar suspension front and rear

Backbone chassis

Horizontally-opposed four

THE POWER PACK

All-alloy construction

Race-specification cylinder heads

Lightened flywheel

Two twin-choke carburetors

Fast flat-four

The stock Beetle engine is not a highly tuned unit. The most powerful factory Beetle is a 1,584-cc unit producing 50 bhp. This engine has been enlarged to 2,398 cc by increasing both bore and stroke. Twin 52-mm two-barrel carbs feed the thirsty engine with gas through a Berg manifold. Race cylinder heads maximize flow and the flywheel has been lightened to reduce reciprocating weight. Very little of the original engine remains but it produces an amazing 210 bhp.

Body beautiful

The beautifully prepared and finished body of this Beetle makes it a real head turner. It's what's under the skin that counts though. The 210-bhp engine propels it to 13-second ¼-mile times, and it is a highly successful drag strip contender.

A large proportion of vintage Beetles have been modified in some form.

Volkswagen BEETLE

This beautiful blue Beetle may look like a mildly modified VW, but it certainly has the performance to match its stunning looks. An engine developing over 200 bhp makes sure of that.

Nerf bars

Instead of the original chrome bumpers, this car has 'nerf bars.' They are a common modification to customized Beetles.

Slick rear tires

Slick rear tires ensure maximum traction off the line. In true budget drag racing style, they are Firestone recapped slicks.

Highly-tuned engine

The flat-four now has a capacity of nearly 2.4 liters and produces an incredible 210 bhp—that's about 180 bhp at the rear wheels. This means this Beetle is capable of covering the ¼-mile in 13 seconds.

Simple interior

The interior has been kept simple. It has original VW weave carpets, Porsche 911 seats retrimmed in blue leather and an original EMPI steering wheel.

Lowered front suspension

This car features a lowered front suspension to achieve the classic nose in the weeds stance. There are Koni shock absorbers in the front and rear.

Porsche rear brakes

In order to help stop this powerful VW from high speed, it is fitted with Porsche 356 rear drums which are much more effective than the standard VW brakes.

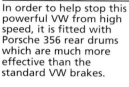

Specifications

1956 Volkswagen Beetle

ENGINE

Type: Flat-four

Construction: Cast-alloy block and heads

Valve gear: Two valves per cylinder operated by a single camshaft via pushrods and rocker

Bore and stroke: 3.70 in. x 3.30 in.

Displacement: 2,398 cc

Compression ratio: 9.5:1

Induction system: Two twin-barrel JayCee 52-mm carburetors

Maximum power: 210 bhp at 7,000 rpm

Maximum torque: 180 lb-ft at 4,800 rpm

Top speed: 133 mph

0-60 mph: 5.2 sec.

TRANSMISSION

Four-speed manual

BODY/CHASSIS

Steel backbone chassis with steel two-door sedan bodyshell

SPECIAL FEATURES

These controls increase the engine's timing from inside the car.

A large, 1¾-inch tailpipe helps expel exhaust gases efficiently.

RUNNING GEAR

Steering: Worm-and-nut

Front suspension: Transverse torsion bars, with parallel trailing arms and telescopic shock absorbers.

Rear suspension: Transverse torsion bars with radius arms and telescopic shock absorbers

Brakes: Discs (front), drums (rear)

Wheels: American Racing, 15-in. dia.

Tires: 145/70-15 (front), 6.00 x 15 (rear)

DIMENSIONS

Length: 165.0 in.   **Width:** 60.9 in.

Height: 61.0 in.   **Wheelbase:** 94.5 in.

Track: 49.8 in. (front), 50.2 in. (rear)

Weight: 1,629 lbs.

Willys **COUPE**

Back in the early 1960s, old pre-war cars were popular as a basis for 'Gasser' Super Stock drag cars. The 1940 Willys was especially popular and gained notoriety in the hands of famous racers.

"...not for the faint-hearted."

"With a supercharged 392-cubic inch Chrysler hemi V8 and a lightweight body, this Willys street machine is not for the faint-hearted. It was built for one reason— going fast in the standing start ¼ mile. The huge rear tires give tremendous bite, and hitting the gas pedal results in the nose heading skyward at launch. Good weight transfer is essential in drag racing and to achieve this any real attempt to make the car handle well has been sacrificed."

Inside, this 1940 Coupe is bright and colorful and features cloth covered seats.

Milestones

1940 Willys

introduces its new 440 series, which includes an elegant little business coupe. Production of this series continues until early 1942.

By 1967 the lighter 33 Willys was the car of choice for B/Gas Super Stock class drag racing.

1949 Sanctioned

drag racing begins. Most competitors run their cars on pump gasoline, although some use nitromethane. Lightweight pre-war cars are popular choices for stock-bodied dragsters.

One of the most famous exponents of the Willys was Jack Merkel, who won at the Indy Nationals in 1964 and 1965.

1960 Gasoline-powered

vehicles now have their own 'Gasser' class. By 1963 the Willys were gaining a monopoly in this class, being among the lightest, and hence fastest, cars available for B/Gas sanctioned drag racing.

UNDER THE SKIN

Tubular steel chassis

Lowered suspension

Custom-fabricated wheel tubs

Big-block V8

Extra strength

To cope with more power than Willys ever intended the car to handle, this 1940s Coupe has a fabricated steel tubular chassis. It features a four-bar link rear suspension with a narrowed 9-inch rear taken from a Lincoln Mk VII. Custom fabricated rear wheel tubs, plus huge Mickey Thompson rear slick tires are fitted for maximum traction.

THE POWER PACK

Exotic powerplant

Introduced in 1951 and displacing 331 cubic inches, the original Chrysler hemi was a revelation. With overhead valves and special hemispherical combustion chambers, it churned out 180 bhp and helped to make Chrysler a force in NASCAR. Bored and stroked to 392 cubic inches until its demise in 1958, it was a popular choice for drag racers running B/Gas Super Stock class in the 1960s. Highly modified versions using a supercharger can produce up to 700 bhp.

Hemispherical combustion chambers

Overhead valves

Cast-iron block and cylinder heads

Deep capacity oil pan

Cult 'Gasser'

Today, the 1940 Willys is one of the most sought-after nostalgia drag cars. Examples which raced in the 1960s are being bought and restored and are once again hitting the strips. With help from modern technology they are faster and safer than ever before.

The early 1940s Willys are now being rediscovered by enthusiasts.

Willys COUPE

Today, Willys are back on the strips. With the benefit of modern technology, these cars are faster than racers back in the 1960s could possibly have imagined.

Narrowed rear end

To accommodate the huge tires, the rear axle has been considerably narrowed.

Custom interior

Inside, there are a full set of gauges, plus gray tweed interior panels and bucket seats.

Scuff plate

During hard take-offs the car's nose lifts off the ground. A scuff plate is fitted under the rear of the chassis to prevent damage.

Skinny front tires

Weight transfer is essential for a good ET (elapsed time) in sanctioned drag racing and therefore many racers find it imperative to make the front end as light as possible. Lightweight wheels and skinny front tires contribute to weight reduction and also help the back tires to grip.

Body trim

Despite being primarily a drag car, this 1940 Willys still retains a substantial amount of trim, including the door handles and the hood ornament.

Dropped suspension

In the 1960s many of these Coupes had high front suspension for better weight transfer. As speeds increased, this became dangerous and dropped set-ups were introduced, giving the driver better control at speed.

Blown hemi V8

Taken from a 1958 Chrysler, the 392-cubic inch hemi has been fitted with a Weiand intake, twin carburetors and a GMC supercharger.

Specifications

1940 Willys Coupe

ENGINE

Type: V8

Construction: Cast-iron block and heads

Valve gear: Two valves per cylinder operated by pushrods and rocker arms

Bore and stroke: 4 in. x 3.90 in.

Displacement: 392 c.i.

Compression ratio: 10.0:1

Induction system: Two Holley carburetors and a GMC 671 supercharger

Maximum power: 700 bhp at 6,800 rpm

Maximum torque: 509 lb-ft at 3,200 rpm

Top speed: 150 mph

0-60 mph: 3.4 sec.

TRANSMISSION

1969 Dodge 727 TorqueFlite with B&M Quick Silver shifter

BODY/CHASSIS

Welded steel and fiberglass body on separate ladder-type frame

SPECIAL FEATURES

The fiberglass hood has a cut-out to fit the supercharger intake.

 A special quick-shifter enables rapid and precise gear shifts, and a full set of gauges keeps the driver informed.

RUNNING GEAR

Steering: Rack-and-pinion

Front suspension: Fabricated tubular wishbones with dropped spindles, cut coil springs and shocks

Rear suspension: Narrowed live axle with custom leaf springs, lowering blocks and telescopic shocks

Brakes: Discs (front and rear)

Wheels: Custom, 5½ x 15 in. (front), 18½ x 15 in. (rear)

Tires: BF Goodrich Defenders (front), Mickey Thompson Pro Sportsman (rear)

DIMENSIONS

Length: 165.5 in. **Width:** 61.2 in.

Height: 57 in. **Wheelbase:** 102 in.

Track: 47.7 in. (front), 41.4 in. (rear)

Weight: 1,872 lbs.

Index